Take Control

to Avoid the Pitfalls of Publishing

Errors Aspiring Authors Make and How to Avoid Them

Dr. Melissa Caudle

Absolute Author
Publishing House

https://absoluteauthorpuplishinghouse.com/

Take Control to Avoid the Pitfalls of Publishing

Publisher: Absolute Publishing House, New Orleans, LA
Editor: Kathy Rabb Kittok
Junior Editor: Paul S. Dupre
Beta Readers: Dr. Carol Michaels, Uma Rajagopal, Rose Roach, G.L. Room, Eugene Cole, Terry Atzen, Kirhonda Williams, and Shawna James
Cover Designer: Rebecca *@RebeccaCovers*
Author Photographer: Robby Cook Stroud
Photographs: All photographs used with permission from Stock Nation

Proudly Printed in the United States of America

Library of Congress Cataloging-in-Publication Data
Caudle, Melissa.
Take Control to Avoid the Pitfalls of Publishing / Dr. Melissa Caudle
p. cm.
ISBN-13:
1. Resource 2. Writing 3. Author Resources 4. Reference

DEDICATION

To all aspiring authors. May you write until your heart's content.

TESTIMONIALS

"Self-publishing is a rewarding task, but can be daunting if you don't have the best team and resources to help you along your publishing journey. Dr. Melissa Caudle has written several books, and she has helped thousands of authors publish. I often tease her by calling her the Midwife of Books because she helped birth my baby, *The Mysteries of Woodland Academy,* into the world. In her new book, *Take Control to Avoid the Pitfalls of Publishing,* Dr. Caudle puts her heart and soul into this self-help book to help new authors and veteran authors publish strong.

I know first-hand how imperative it is to have all the facts and an excellent support team when beginning publication. If I had not found Dr. Melissa Caudle, my novel *The Mysteries of Woodland Academy* wouldn't be published today. Dr. Caudle took me, a first-time author, and made my publishing dream a reality. I didn't know the first thing about publishing, let alone publishing the right way. Along with Absolute Author Publishing House, she helped me become a better writer and author. Dr. Caudle held my hand throughout the process, and she treated my novel as if it was her very own. Dr. Caudle has the experience, expertise, wisdom to help all authors publish their books; she's truly a whiz when it comes to the literary world. Not only is she amazing to work with, but she also has become a wonderful friend. I appreciate her, and I am sure we will work together again... she's simply the best." **K.D. Williams - YA Author of *The Mysteries of Woodland Academy***

"This book is a must-have for authors, particularly those new to this game. I am sure that there are tidbits of info that would be helpful to more seasoned authors, as well. It is like having your own personal teacher guide you through the murky waters of marketing and publishing.

There is also a wealth of knowledge about the actual writing of your manuscript. Especially helpful are the various detailed charts and instructions on how to format your publications. You can literally develop your book from cover to cover, as Dr. Mel details all the inside and outside parts of taking your manuscript from a draft to a finely tuned marketable novel. Dr. Mel leads you on the journey through the difficult publishing stage and teaches you to avoid many pitfalls in the process. YOU NEED THIS!" **Rose Roach – Upcoming Unpublished Author**

"This book is the most comprehensive book for authors available on the market. I couldn't believe the amount of information, from writing tips to character development to creating impactful dialogue; this book is a must-have for every author. Dr. Mel's experience as an author, editor, and publisher is golden. **Jamie Alyson, Author of *Where the Mind Wanders***

"Dr. Caudle has the experience, expertise, and wisdom to help all authors publish, distribute, and market their books; she's truly the guru when it comes to the literary world. Do yourself a favor and purchase this book. You won't be sorry that you did. In the long run, you will save hours and money." **Mark Randolph, Author of *The Darkside of Jupiter***

ACKNOWLEDGMENTS

I would be remiss if I didn't acknowledge those who have supported me on my journey to becoming a bestselling author. There are many, but most importantly, those who support me unconditionally -- my family. Without a doubt, they inspire, encourage, and love me as I am by accepting my creativity. And, when I need to go on a cruise or to the beach, my guilty pleasures, they don't mind allowing me to finish or start a new manuscript.

Next, I want to thank my editing team, Kathy Rabb Kittok and Paul S. Dupre, who make me shine. Both of you are incredibly talented and an asset to Absolute Author Publishing House and me. I can't express my sincere gratitude enough.

I also want to thank my Beta Readers, who provided valuable insight into this manuscript. They include Uma Rajagopal, Rose Roach, G.L. Room, Eugene Cole, Shawna James, Terry Atzen, Kirhonda Williams, and Dr. Carol Michaels. A special shout out to Uma Rajagopal, who helped me develop the final title during a Fiverr coaching session I conducted with her on publishing.

Finally, I want to thank all authors who have crossed my path and trusted me with editing and publishing their books with Absolute Author Publishing House. Because of you, I wrote this book for aspiring authors to navigate the publishing process and avoid the many pitfalls and mistakes new authors make.

TABLE OF CONTENTS

INTRODUCTION

Congratulations! You want to become a published author. That is a milestone, and you should be proud of yourself. Please tell me I caught you before you started your journey in the publishing world. Why? Let me introduce myself. As the owner of Absolute Author Publishing House, senior editor, bestselling author with over ninety books, fiction and nonfiction, and adult and children's books, I speak from experience regarding the pitfalls of publishing and how to avoid them. I have written and published over ninety books, edited over a thousand manuscripts for other authors, formatted books, marketed books, and wrote *How to Launch and Market a Book: The Six Month Countdown* for authors. I think this qualifies me to author this one. I have also worked with hundreds of authors, keeping them from making significant mistakes with distribution and marketing. My clients call me two names -- Boss Lady and The Book Doctor. I'm here to help you with the information I present.

Over the years, I gained tremendous insight into what it takes to become a bestseller and become a published author. I made mistakes and learned from them. As your journey begins, you will discover so many avenues to consider, which can be overwhelming, and unfortunately, there is a massive learning curve that awaits. Look at the list below:

- How long does it take to write a book?
- Do you need a degree to become a published author?
- What genres sell the best?
- What format do you need?
- How important is the backstory?
- How important are the characters?
- How important are the plot and subplots?
- How do you know when the book is finished?
- Who do you turn to for advice or help?
- Can you self-publish?
- Do you need a traditional publisher?
- What does it mean to be published?
- What are the steps to publish?
- What is the difference between publishing and distribution?
- How do you know the best distribution channel for you and your book?
- What is an ISBN?
- Should you accept a free ISBN?
- Do you need an interior designer for your manuscript?
- Is there a difference between an author and a writer?
- When should you create your cover?
- What goes on the cover?
- How do you vet editors?
- How do you find an illustrator?
- How do you format a paperback, hardback, eBook?
- Do you need to do an audiobook?
- Do audiobooks sell?
- Do you need to copyright your book?
- How do you price a paperback?
- How do you price an eBook?

- How do you price a hardback?
- How do you price an audiobook?
- How do you deal with critical reviews?
- Do you need a literary agent?

After reading the questions, you should get the idea that publishing a book is more complex than you might have initially thought. However, you can take control and avoid publishing pitfalls, which are paramount to your success; otherwise, you will waste a tremendous amount of money, time, and resources. Trust me, the frustration can be endless, but this book provides you with solid answers every aspiring author needs unless you're wealthy or have money to burn; keep reading this book. It is filled with tons of information and addresses the common pitfalls of writing, mistakes made during the writing process, the mistakes made in publishing and distribution, and how to fix them before it is too late.

I wish you much success in your journey.

Sincerely,

Dr. Melissa Caudle
www.drmelcaudle.com/
www.drmelmessage.com

CHAPTER ONE

Myths and Misconceptions

In high school and college, my favorite class was creative writing. Something about the writing process and creating characters, backstories, and dialogues entertained me, and I wanted to write more. My teachers and my family considered me a writing machine. Somehow, I was gifted with the art of gab and writing. Writing comes easy for me, and I often feel as if I write in my sleep -- literally. Oddly enough, as a child, I thought everyone could write. Boy, oh boy, was I wrong -- completely wrong! My sisters struggled, my friends struggled, and my classmates struggled to write a single paragraph. Honestly, I didn't understand that. My mistake again.

Since then, and after working with thousands of new and seasoned authors, it became clear they hold on to myths and formed many misconceptions about the art of writing. I want to take the time to review the most critical.

Myths and Misconceptions

1. **When you write, you write alone.** Not so true. How can that be? Easy. When you write, you bring your myriad of experiences. Because of that, you're not alone in your writing

process. How many times when you write have you heard your inner voice repeat what your mother warned you about or something a former lover said to you? What about heated words exchanged during an argument? Do you get flashbacks of meeting a stranger? Do you recall smells, sights, and sounds? So, when you thought you were writing in isolation, you're not. You bring along with you experiences and memories packed away in your luggage or stuffed in a closet; this is absolutely the best thing for writers -- all writers. Without our myriad experiences, we are mere shells spitting out words onto a page that leaves readers disappointed. To bring a character to life, you become that character and all of your characters. Again, you are not alone when you write. Even If you are writing a memoir, you're not alone. You bring your inner voice and experiences with you.

2. **If I write it, they'll read it.** No, no, and no! Here is the pitfall of this thinking. When you write a book, an article, or a blog post, nothing guarantees someone will read it. Gaining a following is a significant task and must be manipulated and navigated to gain momentum. I know; I have almost ten million readers on my blog: www.drmelmessage.com/. Remember, when you publish a book, it means someone may not purchase it, much less read it. The moral of this story is to make sure that you establish or brand yourself as a writer and create the best product capable of competing with sixty million books available on the market.

3. **Most aspiring authors start with their debut novels.** This is so far from the truth it hurts. Authors, especially bestselling ones, have honed their craft over the years. In the seventh grade, I co-wrote my first book, *Sunshine my Love*, with my best friend, Anne Danielson. It was my beginning, and I never looked back. Seasoned authors write, rewrite, edit, rewrite, and write again up to the last minute they publish. Most writers start with a blog, poetry, or a collection of short stories. The more you write, the better writer you become. I guess I can say the same thing about editing. The more you edit, the better you become at it. Of course, as with everything you want to master in life, you must practice, practice, and practice. But wait! Not just practice, but perfect practice. Spending time every day writing is the best writing habit you can develop.

4. **Writing is a hobby.** What! That statement upsets me and makes me cringe. When I first began my career as an author, my family, especially my husband, called my writing nothing more than a hobby. I strongly disagreed. Hobbies are for recreation designed to allow your creativity to flow without the expectation of getting paid. For me, writing is a career, and

it takes dedication to make a career with your writing. If you view writing as your hobby, you'll never master the art. Instead, treat it as an occupation, commit to perfection, and take courses or hire a writing coach like me. In the appendix, I list all of my services: coaching, editing, publishing, distribution, and marketing. Think about it. If you're a nurse, did you start as a nurse, or did you have to go to school? The same as for an electrician, a teacher, a chemist, and so forth. To be a professional, you must train.

5. **You need a vivid imagination to become a professional writer**. No, no, and no! Imagination is key to writing, especially if you are writing fiction. However, not all books are fiction. As an editor and owner of Absolute Author Publishing House, I have helped thousands of authors reach their dream. Sure, writing children's books and fiction requires imagination and creativity. Your story has to come from somewhere and from inspiration. Now consider autobiographies, self-help books, religious discourse, journals, and more. Those aren't fiction and are usually written by a professional with experience in that field if they want any credibility with their audience. The

best example is this book. I have written and published dozens of books, but this one is a self-help book for authors. Without my experience as CEO of Absolute Author Publishing House (AAPH), senior editor, award-winning screenwriter, and a #1 New Release author with over ninety books, do you think you would have confidence in the knowledge I share? I think not. I bring tons of expertise in writing and publishing. So, if you want to share your knowledge, you can write a book that does not require imagination.

6. **Publishing a book is very expensive.** Wait! Not so true anymore, but you have to be careful. Not all is as it seems. There are a lot of scams, and you must be cautious before jumping headfirst into a contract with a company. Here is what I mean by that. The most expensive cost of writing is your time. I am frequently asked how long it takes for me to write a book. If that isn't a setup type of question, I don't know what one is. There is no fixed amount of time to write a book. My novel, *The Keystroke Killer: Transcendence,* took eight weeks to write. However, it took me a year for the editing and beta reading process before I published it. My children's book, *The Creek Dweller in the Bayou,* took me twelve hours to write, one week to edit, four weeks to vet illustrators, and eight more weeks for the illustrations to be added to my manuscript. The cost factor in publishing occurs with the price of formatting, editing, copyright filing, illustrations, graphics, and getting the ISBNs ready to publish. The prices vary according to who you use. Hold tight; I'll go into more detail later about these areas and how to get the best value for your money.

7. **I'm going to get rich when I publish my book, and I can quit my day job.** This is so far from the truth. First, most new authors don't make a lot of money with their first book. Again, it takes time to formulate your reputation and brand yourself as an established author. The more I write and publish, the

easier it is to sell my books. So, please don't go into this thinking you will give up your day job anytime soon. It is rare to become an instant millionaire with your first book.

8. **I need a book deal to become a published author.** This myth drives me crazy. Why? First, there are many opportunities for publishing a book, including self-publishing, traditional publishing, vanity press publishing, or a hybrid combination. Again, I will go into more detail in a later chapter.

9. **To write fiction, I need to have a muse.** No, again, and that is a myth. However, often writers will have a muse or two. I get my inspiration from people watching, especially on a cruise ship, or I dream up a character and mold them into interesting, intriguing, and slightly different from the norm. Who wants a boring character? Not me.

10. **You need specific software to write a book.** Nope! Most publishers only accept a Microsoft Word document. I use Word for all of my manuscripts, and I also use it when I format a book. With that said, there is plenty of software available,

but if I were you, I'd save my money and put it toward something else.

11. **Anyone can be a professional writer.** Not so true, I'm sorry. If you lack basic grammar skills and can't spell, it is challenging to finish your first draft. I have seen many authors give up when they could have sought help from a developmental editor or writing coach. So, the moral of this story, don't give up, focus, and hone your craft.

12. **If my novel is a bestseller and is good, it will be made into a movie.** You better think this one through before you get disappointed. Several things have to happen for a novel to be considered for a movie. It must have the momentum behind it, a screenplay adapted from it, and then the screenplay sold. Still, that doesn't mean it will be an instant success or made into a movie. Please remember that writing a screenplay is a different beast from writing a novel, and most screenwriters spent years honing their craft long before they sold a screenplay. So, before you get that vision of grandeur, set realistic expectations.

13. **To be an author, I need to have a literary agent.** Nope, again. Unless they are famous, most authors don't have a literary agent. And remember, you don't need to have one either. Nowadays, literary agents are scarce, and the chances of obtaining one are slim if you are self-published.

14. **I can bypass hiring a professional editor because my friends and family have agreed to do it for me.** Big mistake in this line of thinking. Friends and family can't do what a professional editor can. Editing a manuscript for a book has its own set of rules. Chicago Manuel and APA rules fly out the window. A great editor is worth their weight in gold.

15. **The more I read, the better writer I become.** Many authors believe this to be true, but it is only a myth. The more you read, the better reader you become. Why? Not all books are created the same. If you read many books, which are poorly written, you learn that and mimic those errors. Therefore, when reading, just for fun, do that. Yes, identify what you like about a writing style and what drives you crazy. Then practice writing by writing and not by reading.

16. **The more verbose I am in my writing, the better it will be received.** This couldn't be further from the truth. If you write a book and have too much verbiage, it will backfire on you. The same holds for using words that no one knows the definition. Readers don't want to read a novel or a memoir where they have to look up words to obtain the meaning constantly. Instead, they won't read the book at all. The best case I can think of is a novel that I edited, and the author worked in artificial intelligence. His way of thinking was precise in defining artificial intelligence; it was boring. No one cares. They care about the character, or in this case, the robot. Readers didn't need to know the science behind artificial intelligence to enjoy the story. I had the author rewrite the entire novel in layman's terms, and it turned out to be a bestseller. Here, less was more, and the more succinct the author became in their writing, the more engaging the character became.

17. **I should write a book about my life because it is interesting.** So what? If you believe this, you need a reality check. Yes, your life may be filled with exciting events and experiences, but if readers don't care about it, they won't read it. When you write about your life, you need to set an end game -- how will the reader benefit, and what can they learn from your life's story? Think about that. My case is that I had an author I worked with during the developmental stage of writing. The author's background was fascinating, and she had a lot to offer. She had

been kidnapped and sold into sex trafficking when she was twelve. At twenty-six, she escaped. Her journey was compelling and had all the makings for an extraordinary memoir or even take those events and create a novel from it. However, she could never connect the dots, and she was all over the place jumping from one event to the other, never really getting to the meat of the situation. It was boring. With my help, we turned it into something fantastic, and when it was all said and printed, she started a foundation to help other victims. The book became a success.

18. **I don't need to bother with social media to become a successful author.** The worst thing you can do as an author is not to have a social media presence. Where do you think you will get your readers? How will you promote your book? How will others find out about it? A harsh reality is that every year, nearly 800,000 books are published. Do you know what that means? You will be entering a highly competitive market. Without a social media presence, it won't be easy.

19. **I can easily sell my book in a bookstore.** Not so fast and not so easy. First, you cannot be self-published to be considered for placement in a bookstore or library. Let me repeat; you cannot sell your book in bookstores. Sorry if that burst your happy bubble. The fact is retailers don't enjoy buying from Amazon and seek other avenues to obtain the book at a retailer discount. Do your research. Lastly, managers of bookstores tell me they don't have room on their shelves for self-published authors.

20. **I can buy an ISBN from Bowker and won't be self-published.** This is the biggest myth of them all. Yes, you can certainly purchase an ISBN from Bowker. Still, unless you have formed a publishing company, have a corporation listed as a publisher,

and a business license for the company, you are still self-published.

21. **Once my book is published, I can forget about it, and it will sell itself.** Big, big mistake if you believe this. If you think writing and publishing a book is challenging, wait until you get to the marketing and distribution. Be actively involved.

22. **I don't have to copyright my book because I can show a chain of ownership.** Wrong, again. Under no circumstances should you ever publish a book without it being registered with the U.S. Library of Congress. Don't try to save money by skipping this vital step or using the old-fashioned method of mailing the manuscript to yourself. This is not a viable solution.

TIP 1: An ISBN is different from filing your copyright with the U.S. Library of Congress. As the author, you need both for your book. Always read the fine print and your diligence in researching the importance of an ISBN from a publishing company. Also, never accept a free ISBN, or you may lose your distribution rights.

CHAPTER TWO

The Art of Writing

Many writers began their journey early in life. They wrote short stories, created poetry, and wrote essays in grade school, which are great building blocks to becoming a professional writer. Is it enough, though? Sorry to burst your bubble again, but early writing doesn't guarantee your writing success. First, you must learn the art of writing. Gustave Flaubert says, "The art of writing is the art of discovering what you believe." I believe that when you write, it defines your thoughts. Therefore, the more articulate you are, the better writer you become, and you discover the art of writing. My motto is, "When I don't write, I don't feel right."

Writing as an Art

Let's begin by defining the art of writing. The art of writing includes all activities leading up to when you sat down and began writing, including your basic education from kindergarten through the twelfth grade. I bet you would have paid closer attention to your English teachers if you knew you were going to author a book someday. There is nothing better than having a solid grammar, spelling, and punctuation background. So now what? What if you have poor grammar skills? Not to worry, that is what classes and writing coaches accomplish. You must start somewhere. May I suggest taking a course in creative writing from either your local junior college or a four-year university? You don't have to major in English or complete a degree. The goal is to hone your writing skills, and unfortunately, the only way to do that is by learning and then applying what you have learned.

If taking classes isn't an option for you, you're not out of luck or left in limbo. In my city, we have several writer groups where authors can get feedback and swap their writing samples with others to learn from them. I strongly encourage that. If one isn't available near you, start one. You might be surprised by the interest level.

Another avenue is to form the same type of group using Zoom or another video chat conferencing site. I often coach small groups on Zoom, limiting the number to six authors at a time. Keep that in mind when you either join a group or start one. Here, larger isn't better because writers won't get their desired feedback. If you are interested in either group or one-on-one coaching, email me at drmelcaudle@gmail.com.

Improving Your Writing Skills

To improve your writing skills, you must write. Occasionally writing when you have the time will not cut it. You must write every day and rewrite what you write. Sorry, there are no shortcuts. Essentially, practicing writing won't make you a better writer. You must write, learn from your mistakes, and apply your skills. When coaching someone on writing, I use a simple approach -- show me what you have. By this, I want to see their raw writing samples, and then I design my lessons using what they have written. I'm not a proponent of giving exercise worksheets filled with circling grammar mistakes or identifying the correct usage of a word. Rather, the material must come from the writer to learn and master writing and define your art of writing. That's how we learn to be better writers.

Does Reading Improve Your Writing?

One would think that the more you read, the better of a writer you become. Not so much. Reading bestselling authors is important as long as you go into the reading session to obtain knowledge or skill. For instance, I have a unique writing style -- I don't use dialogue tags. You know those pesky endings of he said, or she said. To me, they are useless. I loathe them, and they impede my reading enjoyment. So, when I wrote my first novel, I promised myself that I would not use dialogue tags. How is this possible? Easier than you might think, and I will dedicate an entire section to this later in this book on how not to use dialogue tags. For now, know that just because every writer uses them, including J. K. Rowling, James Patterson, and John Grisham, doesn't mean you need to. That's the beauty of the art of writing. You get to develop your style and be you and not become a copycat writer.

Setting up Your Writing Environment

The more you write, the more you'll want to write. Can you write anywhere? Yes, but should you? That answer depends on you and how you like your environment. For me, I can write anywhere. Oh, happy day! I have dozens of books, and most I finished while on a cruise ship or at the beach. Something about me being around the salt air nourishes my writing creativity. I love that part of my job because I am not looking at the same four walls as I sit behind my desk. That's not to say I don't write in my office. Most of my drafts and rewrites are done in my office -- my writing environment.

When I wrote my first novel, I was in the seventh grade. It was a writing assignment for my English class, and my best friend and I took on this project together. It was a lot of fun. When we wrote, we were in her bedroom or mine. There wasn't any other place to write together, other than the school library, which the librarian discouraged us because we had to talk out our plot and characters.

I must say I have come a long way. Today, my office is in my house, and it is very lovely and large, overlooking the pool in my backyard. Yes, still near water. When I enter my office, I am already in the mindset of writing. I work off three screens, making it easier to navigate the manuscript when cutting and pasting or moving paragraphs and chapters. Somehow, my office sets my tone for my writing day, which usually consists of spending the first thirty minutes answering emails and attending to bills, etc. Then, I set aside at least two hours to concentrate on my writing. This is important as I also own Absolute Author Publishing House and edit others' manuscripts. If I didn't set the time for my writing, I doubt it would finish any book I write at all. That is why it's vital to establish a writing routine in a specific environment.

If you don't have space in your home for a private office, that doesn't mean you can't establish an area. In the early 80s, when I began writing, I turned a walk-in closet into a writing area. That lasted until I became pregnant and needed that closet for the baby things. So, I then set up a small TV tray in the corner of my bedroom with an IBM Selectric typewriter. Do you even know what that is? This is what I had to use before computers. It wasn't easy, but I accomplished the task.

Some authors set up their writing spaces in halls, the kitchen, formal living rooms, or any large enough space to accommodate their computers. With that said, one of my author clients only writes in their living room sitting on the sofa using their laptop. So, I guess what I am trying to convey is it is essential you have an area that you feel comfortable writing.

Does your environment have to be quiet? Not at all. When I write, I have music playing in the background. Somehow, that makes me relax, and the words fly onto the page. Another client of mine can't write unless the television is on. Some say that would be distracting -- not for her. The silence distracts her, not the noise.

The key to your environment is what makes you comfortable enough to write, and you enjoy being there. So, when setting up your environment, consider:

- ✓ **Dedicated workspace.** Choose the area in your home you feel you can be the most productive.

- ✓ **Have a comfortable chair.** There is nothing worse than sitting and writing all day and being uncomfortable. Oh, I don't use a standard desk or executive chair. Instead, I have a leather recliner that sits on an elevated platform. It is comfortable for my writing purposes.

- ✓ **Writing tools.** Have the writing tools close at hand, including pens, pencils, highlighters, printer, printer paper, and sticky notes.

- ✓ **Power outlets.** Ensure that the room has enough electrical outlets to power your printer, computer, and a charging station for your phone and/or IPAD.

- ✓ **Place to post things.** Consider hanging a dry eraser board for outlining or making To-do lists. They come in handy when you get interrupted during your writing process.

- ✓ **Writing resources.** Keep on hand a dictionary and a thesaurus. Yes, you can access both on a computer, but you can often flip through the dictionary and get inspiration when you are stuck for a word.

- ✓ **De-clutter your environment.** Keep your writing area free of clutter. This is more difficult than it sounds as drafts pile up, water glasses, coffee mugs, writing books, and so much more. Every evening, I clean my office as if I expect someone famous to drop by. I wouldn't want to be embarrassed by having a mess. Then, every morning, I have a fresh, clean office to begin my day.

- ✓ **Make your environment welcoming.** Make the environment as personable and as welcoming as possible. I have my artwork on the walls and art completed by my grandchildren. I also keep candles handy and burn them according to need. If I need to calm down, I'll burn a lavender calendar; if I need a pick-me-up scent, my go-to is citrus. If I am writing a sex scene... don't ask. Just kidding. For the more complex scenes, I love the scent of gardenias. I also have a jellyfish tank. No, not real jellyfish, but they look like it, and when I turn on the air bubbles in the tank, the jellyfish change colors and float, which relaxes me.

CHAPTER THREE

What Genre Sells Best

I can't tell you how many times as a publisher I am asked, "What genre sells best?" Honestly, there is a ranking system, but I wouldn't let that deter you from writing in the many literary styles available. What is important is whatever genre you choose as your literary style, you're comfortable with it and have the mindset that there isn't any other that you want to write. That's not to say that you can't cross genres; I do it all the time. However, when writing your manuscript, own, cherish, and believe in that genre.

Types of Literary Genres

Fiction

- **Drama** – Stories filled with dialogue, action, conflict, and emotion.

- **Erotica** – Stories written to present sexual intimacy or those that go against the standard norms.

- **Fable** – A story usually told through animals speaking like humans and having a legendary or supernatural element.

- **Fairy Tale** – Stories usually written for children with a magical creature or fairies in them.

- **Fantasy** – Stories that supersede reality and create strange new worlds and characters. Characters and settings can defy the typical odds – the grass can be blue, and the sky green.

- **Fiction in Verse** – Stories where the narrative is presented in blank verse form, which is where unrhyming verse in iambic pentameter lines is the key.

- **Folklore** – Stories handed down by word of mouth through several generations. This includes songs, myths, and proverbs.

- **Historical Fiction** – Stores based in a historical setting featuring fictional characters or historical events.

- **Horror** – Stories that evoke fear, doom, and scare tactics to engage the reader.

- **Humor** – Written to entertain and make people laugh.

- **Legend** – Like folklore, legends are handed down but are usually based on a national or folk hero. Again, the author stretches the facts to enhance the storyline.

- **Mystery** – Stories solving a crime or unraveling a series of events to solve a murder or other significant crime.

- **Mythology** – Stories dealing with actions of the gods told in a narrative or legend. These are usually based on historical events but will use symbolism for human behavior or a natural event.

- **Poetry** – Authors use verse, imagery, and rhythmic prose, creating an emotional response through imagery.

- **Religious/Inspirational** – Stories with religious tones based on theology.

- **Romance** – Stories where boy meets girl, they fall in love, complications arise, they fall in love again, and they either live happily ever after or go their separate ways.

- **Science Fiction** – Stories are usually set on other planets, based on the future, and use imagined or natural science. These stories may or may not contain creatures or aliens from outer space.

- **Short Story** – Stories of less than ten pages where the action swiftly occurs. Usually, there are no subplots to these stories because of the brevity in writing.

- **Tall Tale** – Stories with no rules, filled with unbelievable heroes who can easily achieve the impossible.

Nonfiction

- **Biography/Autobiography** – Stories which are based on a real person.

- **Essay** – A composition where the author shares their perspective and opinions.

- **Narrative Nonfiction** – A story written based on factual information but reads like fiction.

- **Speech** – The author writes discourse to present during a public address.

Genres That Sell

Before you delve into writing your first manuscript, thinking about the genre that interests you the most is key. You must be true to that genre because readers maintain high expectations. Sometimes, authors write in the bestselling genres to sell more copies. That isn't necessarily a poor plan, but it shouldn't be the main reason for writing in that genre. Your writing usually becomes lackluster if you aren't committed and don't have an interest in that genre. That brings us to the question, "What genre sells the best?"

According to the U.S. Library of Congress and the U.S. Library Association, five genres are listed as bestselling.

- **Romance/Erotica** – Coming in at $1.5 billion in sales each year, topping off the bestselling genre is romance and erotica.

- **Crime/Mystery** – Nearing almost $900 million in sales each year, novels present a crime and solve it.

- **Religious/Inspirational** – Coming in third, at $750 million in sales each year, are the nonfiction books that are religious or inspirational. Gaining speed are novels with religious undertones for both adults and youth.

- **Fantasy/Science Fiction** – With over $650 million in sales each year, fantasy and science fiction genre novels are the fourth bestselling books.

- **Horror/Psychological Thriller** – Although very popular in several circles, books in the horror or psychological genre sell well but lack the total sales coming in at number five, with about $90 million in sales each year.

Now you know the answer. Does this mean you start your first novel or short story as a romance or erotica? That's up to you. My best advice is to love the genre you choose to write. It will be with you for a very long time.

CHAPTER FOUR

Before You Write

Okay, you've picked your genre, and you're excited about writing your debut book. Do you begin by outlining your content? If so, how do you go about it? Do you use index cards? Sticky notes? A dry eraser board? I can make a case for all. The goal is to establish a roadmap to writing your first draft. Trust me; this is easier said than done. It also depends on the genre you have chosen. With a memoir, a chronological outline works exceptionally well. I enjoy using the beat sheet I developed with fiction, which I'll share in the next couple of pages. The point I am making is for you to establish parameters so that your manuscript is fully developed. In the rest of this chapter, I discuss the two techniques mentioned above, followed by the most common formatting issues new authors make and how to avoid them.

Parts of a Book

Here is a lesson for you to define your book. Did you know that there are three parts to every book?

1. **The Front Matter** – includes the title page, copyright page, table of contents, dedication, forward, and prologue.

2. **The Content** – includes the introduction and the remaining chapters in the manuscript.

3. **The Back Matter** – includes about the author, appendix, and index. I also always include the first chapters of several of my books as a way to gain a following and tell the readers about my other books.

These areas drive your manuscript's layout and interior design and must be considered before writing the first word. Unfortunately, many new authors make a mistake at the beginning of the writing process by NOT formatting their manuscript to book industry standards. As an editor and publisher, this drives me crazy. In the beginning, I can understand that authors are putting their thoughts together and, therefore, aren't concerned. However, if you plan your contents using the three-section concept and format your book before you write the first word, you get a better sense of what the final book will look like. So, with this in mind, let's learn to format before you write.

Front Matter Formatting

How to Format the Title Page

When creating your Title page, there are rules. First, there are two styles for a title page -- half page and full page. The half-page consists only of the book's title and nothing more. Whereas a full page, which I prefer for my publishing company, consists of the title, author, and publishing company. Here is how to format your title page to industry standards:

1. Start your title four to six spaces from the top. Give yourself plenty of space. Ideally, the title will be listed using a 16-font size, followed by the subtitle of either 14-font or 13-font size. You can use a different font style or add color according to your preference.

2. This is optional, but if you have special artwork you want to appear on your title page, place it beneath the subtitle.

3. Space down six more and add your name as the author.

4. Beneath your name and a couple of spaces down, you can type in your publishing company or leave it blank. This is up to individual authors.

Sample full page title page.

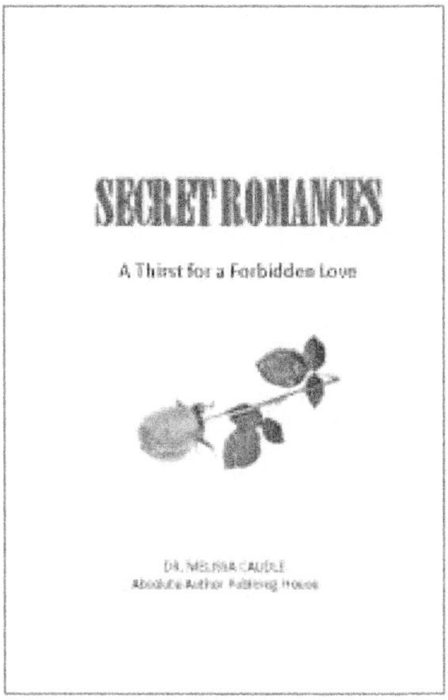

How to Format Your Copyright Page

Your Copyright page is critical because it contains your rights and permission, identifies the contributors, editor, publisher, and Library of Congress In-Publication-Data, including the ISBN. It also tells the readers that the book is not in the public domain, providing your manuscript protection. When you copyright your book, you are protecting your intellectual property, and, as such, it cannot be copied without your permission. All books must have this. Here are the benefits of applying for a copyright with the United States Library of Congress.

1. It provides proof of ownership of the intellectual property.

2. It gives you an added layer of protection for your contents.

3. It discourages others from plagiarism because they know you have registered your material.

What is on the Copyright Page?

A Copyright page includes a myriad of elements. However, not every copyright page contains all -- copyright notice (required).

1. Rights reserved notice (required)
2. ISBN
3. Disclaimers
4. Permissions notice
5. Credits
6. Print edition (usually left off unless a second edition)
7. In-Publication-Data block
8. Ordering information (often for group orders)
9. Author's website or contact information
10. Trademarks (if you have any)
11. Publisher information

How to Format Your Copyright Page

1. If you have a publisher or plan on self-publishing, the logo goes at the top of the page and is centered. For example, here is my Children's Division logo.

Absolute Author
Publishing House
CHILDREN'S DIVISION

2. Space down two spaces and, using Justified text, place the title and italicize it.
3. Beneath the title is reserved for your copyright.
4. Type in ALL RIGHTS RESERVED or the All Rights statement.
5. Next, formulate your disclaimer statement. Please know that there are a variety of disclaimer statements according to the genre. If a publisher publishes you, they usually provide their disclaimer statement; otherwise, it is best to contact an entertainment attorney to draft yours.
6. Space down two spaces and identify the contributors, which usually include the publisher, editor, cover designer, illustrator, if you have one, and credit for author photograph.
7. Create your Library of Congress In-Publication-Data. There is a trick to this, and it must match, or it won't be considered an industry standard. (See picture below). This area includes the book's title, your name, measurements, ISBN(s), and genre.

Please note that it is up to the author to file for the copyright and not the publisher. With that said, filing for the copyright can be burdensome, and you must be exact when doing so to avoid having to pay twice. As a publisher, I offer a gig on Fiverr to file the copyright for you if you need help. All of my gigs are listed in the Appendix. Lastly, please know that filing a copyright and obtaining your ISBN are two different procedures. One does not supplant the other. Many new authors make this mistake thinking once they have obtained the ISBN, they are protected. Not so. The ISBN is the number given to a specific title/format for sale. Here is an example of a copyright page formatted to industry standards.

Absolute Author
Publishing House

Secret Romances
Copyright© 2021
Dr. Melissa Caudle

All rights reserved, including the right to reproduce this book or portions thereof in any form whatsoever—contact author at drmelcaudle@gmail.com or www.drmelcaudle.com.

This book is a work of fiction. Names, characters, places, and incidents are products of the author's imagination or used fictitiously. Any resemblance to actual events, locales, or persons living or dead, is entirely coincidental. Scripture quotations are taken from the New International Version (2018) and used with permission.

Publisher: Absolute Author Publishing House
Project Editor: Dr. Carol Michaels
Developmental Editor: Jamie Dwyer
Final Proof Editors: Kathy Rabb Kittok and Pual Dupre
Copy Editor: Erin Wright
Graphics, Cover, and Back Page: Created by Rebecca@RebeccaCovers
Author Photographer: Robby Cook Stroud

Library of Congress Cataloging-in-Publication Data
Caudle, Melissa
Secret Romances / Dr. Melissa Caudle
p. cm.
ISBN-978-948652-335-1

1. Romance 2. Women's Literature 3. Comedy Romance

---

0 1 2 3 4 5 6 7 8 9
Printed in the United States of America

How to Format Your Dedication Page

On your Dedication page, there is no right or wrong way. I will usually center the word "Dedication" for my company and then use a paragraph style, justified, for the remarks. Often authors will use the center style, but it is not an acceptable industry standard, so avoid doing so as it is a mark of an amateur writer.

DEDICATION

This novel is for my mother, daughters, and granddaughter. May we always find our true loves and live our lives to the fullest.

How to Format Your Acknowledgment Page

Writing a book requires a great deal of support from family, friends, mentors, editors, and publishers. Your Acknowledgment page is the perfect spot to recognize each one. Some authors will write a single sentence, whereas others will write paragraphs. Again, this is up to each author and whom they decide they want to recognize.

Acknowledgment

Many people inspired me to author this book, and I wish to acknowledge them.

First and foremost, my daughter Jamie Alyson who helped me to create the characters and the plot. The inspiration for this novel came in 2005 when she and I lived in Orange Beach, Alabama, after Hurricane Katrina. We were two girls all alone while my husband remained in New Orleans to rebuild our home. It was during this time that we came up with the characters and the plot. Thank you, Jamie, for your creativity.

Second, my husband Mike who is the backbone of my life, keeping our home in order, the pool ready for a swim, and the endless gourmet meals he prepared.

Third, my family, who always encourage me to pursue my writing and have supported me through all my early endeavors.

Fourth, Tina Rubin, my best friend, thank you for the wine and the time you spent reviewing the first, second, and final edition of this novel.

Fifth, to my editing team from Absolute Author Publishing House: Kathy Rabb Kittok and Dr. Carol Michaels, whom I always welcome your edits, feedback, and comments.

Sixth, I'd like to thank Rebecca of RebbecaCovers for her beautiful design of the front and back jacket of this book

Finally, to my focus group members, I value your opinions, and I'm grateful for your insight and your time and support. In no particular order, the focus group members included: Sally Mayfield, Loretta Pines, Tammy Boudreaux, Sandra Belington, Sasha Standford-Smith, Helen V. Ray and Diane Lang.

Although the Table of Contents is in the front matter of your book, it is not usually formatted until all of your chapters have been created, and your final editing is completed.

TIP 2: Be sure to spell acknowledgment and foreward correctly.

How to Format Your Middle Section

First, it is important to know that most editors, publishers, and literary agents have specific formatting stipulations. Therefore, you must understand their specifications before you write. My company established ours, which meets or exceeds industry standards. The following is what we require.

1. **Set the Font.** Times New Roman, 12-point, is the industry standard because it is easy on the eyes for reading purposes. If that is your goal, avoid using a crazy or different font because it won't be accepted by a traditional publisher or a literary agent. When it comes down to interior design, that is when you can modify your fonts for emphasis, and not before. The second, third, and fourth accepted fonts are Arial, Calibri, and Palapento Linotype. Look at the differences in the four fonts side by side.

Fonts can change everything when writing.
(Times New Roman)

Fonts can change everything when writing.
(Arial)

Fonts can change everything when writing.
(Calibri)

Fonts can change everything when writing.
(Palapento Linotype)

Notice in the examples each font and the amount of line space it takes for each sentence. The most obvious is that less space is used for Times New Roman. Ideally, this is used because using less space when writing lowers the printing cost because the number of pages decreases. That is why most publishers and distributors use Times New Roman. So, if your goal is to make more on each copy of your book, I recommend you stick with Times New Roman or Calibri.

2. **Page Dimensions.** Set your page settings to the size of the book before writing the first word. That way, you have a better idea of what your book will look like and the number of pages when you complete your first draft. The standard page sizes, in inches, for books, according to the genre, are:

    ✓ **Fiction:** 4.25 x 6.87, 5 x 8, 5.25 x 8, 5.5 x 8.5, 6 x 9
    ✓ **Novella:** 5 x 8
    ✓ **Children's:** 7.5 x 7.5, 7 x 10, 10 x 8
    ✓ **Textbooks:** 6 x 9, 7 x 10, 8.5 x 11
    ✓ **Non-fiction:** 5.5 x 8.5, 6 x 9, 7 x 10
    ✓ **Memoir:** 5.25 x 8, 5.5 x 8.5
    ✓ **Photography:** Whatever you see fit!

    To set the page size in Word, go to set Layout in Word, go to size, and look at the drop-down menu and either find the size you want or manually input the size.

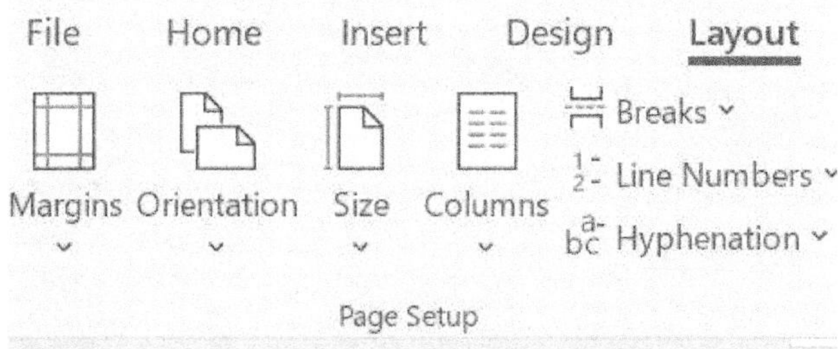

You can choose paper, margins, or layout in the Page Setup area. To set the page size, set the width and the height to the size of your book.

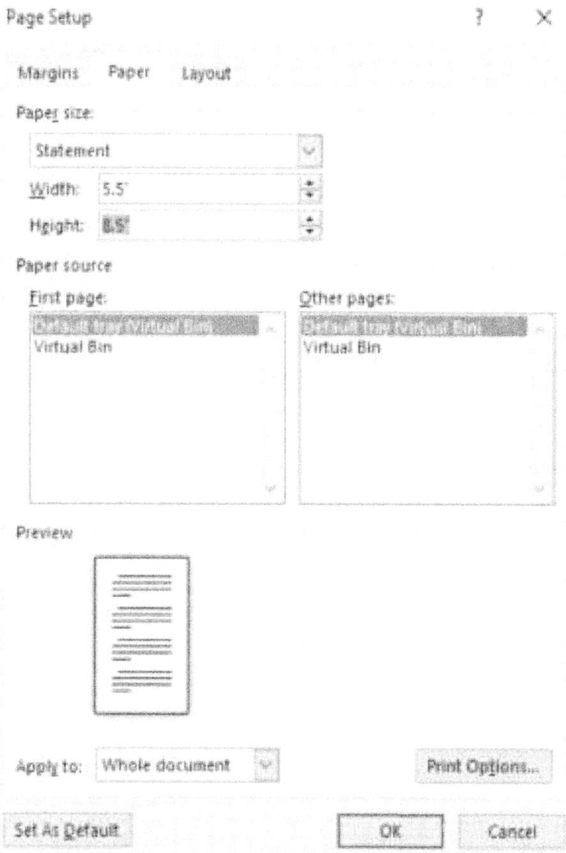

To set margins in Word, go to Layout, and click on the arrow beneath Margins. I recommend using .5 or .7 for all margins, headers, and footers. Many authors will set the margins at 1.0. I recommend that you never set your margin lower than .5 because it will cause problems for you during the printing process. Also, remember if you plan to use a header for your book title, the margin size defines how much room you will have for it.

Note: You may also set the page, including the margins and size, by accessing it using the lower arrow on the right. See the image below.

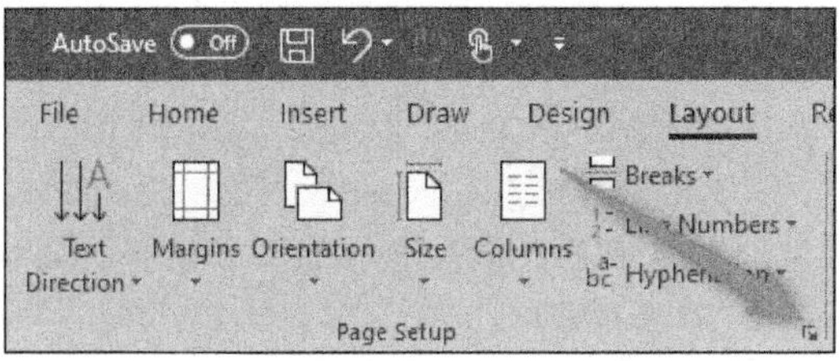

3. **Alignment.** Here is where new authors make their mistakes. They try to center things. DON'T. Instead, you will need to choose between a left justified or full justified. Here is the difference.

   Left Justified Example

   > When writing a book, especially during the first draft stage, margins can either be left justified or full justified.

   Justified Example

   > When writing a book, especially during the first draft stage, margins can either be left justified or full justified.

   There is no correct answer but an author's preference. My preference is using the full justified because I like the clean lines it presents.

4. **Single Space.** Many authors have a problem with this area, especially those of us over fifty who were taught to double-space after periods. This is no longer the case and should be avoided. It is critical that you only use one space after each end punctuation mark.

   With paragraphs, you can either have a single space between the paragraphs and not indent the first line or no space between paragraphs and indent the paragraph. Again, both are correct and usually are the author's preference or according to the genre. For example, most fiction authors use indented paragraphs without full paragraph breaks, whereas nonfiction authors use full justified with non-indent paragraphs, as I do in this book. If you're uncertain about the format you like, go to Amazon, and use the Look Inside feature of different books in your genre. That is the best measure for you to determine the style you like.

5. **Page Breaks.** At the end of each chapter, use page breaks rather than spacing down to create a new page. This is a simple process by clicking on **Insert>Break>Page Break** in Word's Top Menu.

6. **Page Numbers.** Numbering your pages and when to start creates havoc for new writers. First, new authors start their page numbering on the title page and continue to the end. This is wrong. Earlier, I discussed the book's three parts, e.g., front matter, content, and back matter. Each of these sections needs to be marked using the Layout and creating section breaks. Here are the general rules:

    1. The front matter does not get page numbers, including the title page, copyright page, acknowledgments, dedication, and table of contents.

    2. The content section includes the preface or introduction and the chapters of each book. The introduction or preface is numbered using Roman numerals in lowercase, whereas chapters use numbers 1.

    3. The back matter consists of Appendix, Index, About the Author, are numbered but are a continuation of the numbering from the content.

To place page numbers in Word, double-click within the page's header area where your story begins and click **Insert > Page**

Numbers, then select your preferred options. Next, choose to place your page numbers in the center at the bottom in the footer section.

7. **Title Header.** Two things are needed in the header -- the book's title begins on the first chapter, and your name is on the next page. In addition, the title is usually all caps, while the author's name only capitalizes the first initial of their first and last name.

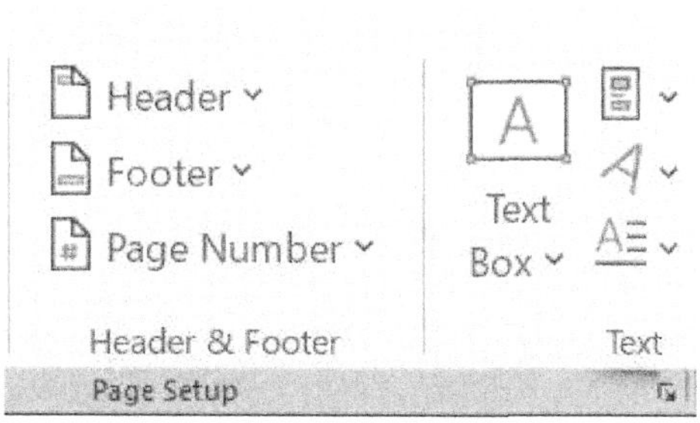

8. **Table of Contents.** Not all books require a Table of Contents. Please keep this in mind. Don't fall into the trap you must because other authors create them. Always remember that this is your book. Here are five benefits of creating a Table of Contents.

    1. **Provides a bird's-eye view.** At a glance, once created, a Table of Contents allows the reader to easily view the contents and flow from one chapter to the next.
    2. **The book looks more professional.** Readers are spoiled, and they are used to looking at a book formatted to industry standards.
    3. **Provides a roadmap for the author.** When you create a Table of Contents, it is a way to outline your book, providing a roadmap until completion.

4. **Provides a focal point for readers and reviewers to discuss each chapter.** You've heard the old saying, "A picture is worth a thousand words." Here, the Table of Contents is that picture. By glancing at the Table of Contents, readers in a discussion group, a book club can easily find and locate each chapter or topic for discussion.

5. **Provides hyperlinks in an eBook.** When used in an eBook, the chapters will be hyperlinked so a reader can return to the last spot they were reading.

How to Create a Table of Contents

1. First, you must mark your Table of Content entries by choosing **References**, highlighting what you want included, and Add Text marking the intended level. Once everything is marked, you can create the Table of Contents.

   Once you have marked everything, proceed to the next step.

   Note: I usually mark the chapter number as Level 1 and the chapter title as Level 2.

2. Place your cursor where you want to add the Table of Contents in your manuscript.

3. Go to **References** > **Table of Contents** and choose an automatic style. Then click on it. Your Table of Contents will automatically be generated.

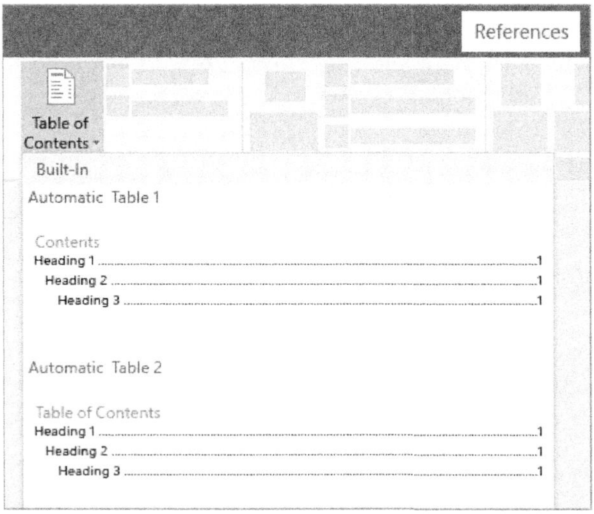

4. If you change your document that affects the Table of Contents, you can easily update it by right-clicking the Table of Contents and choosing **Update Field**.

   If you have missing entries, you did not format the headings as such. Instead, for each heading you want to be included, select the heading text by going to Home > Styles and choosing **Heading 1**.

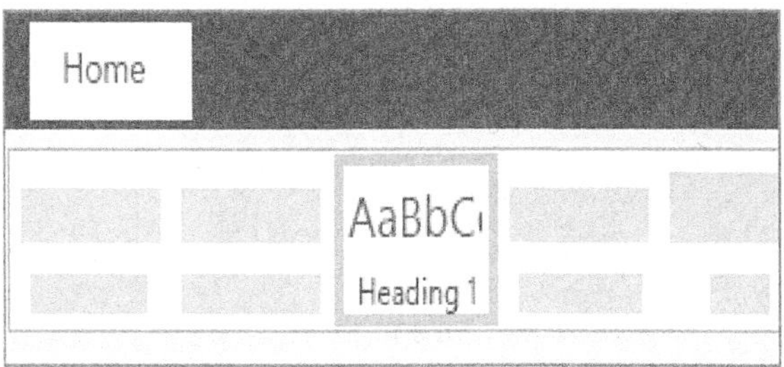

Then update the Table of Contents. You can accomplish this two ways -- by only choosing to update the page numbers or updating the entire Table. Notice the layout below where it says **Update Table**.

Practice, Practice, Practice

Now, try it. Open your Microsoft Word software and try formatting your first manuscript. I suggest starting with a blank document and formatting. Then, if you have a manuscript that you have started, try formatting that. Start with the front matter, format several chapters, and add the About the Author section at the back. The more you practice, the better you become at formatting.

I include a sample Title page, Copyright page, Table of Contents, and headers and footers from several of my books for your reference. On the next page are samples of the Title and Copyright page from my novel *A.D.A.M. The Beginning of Life*.

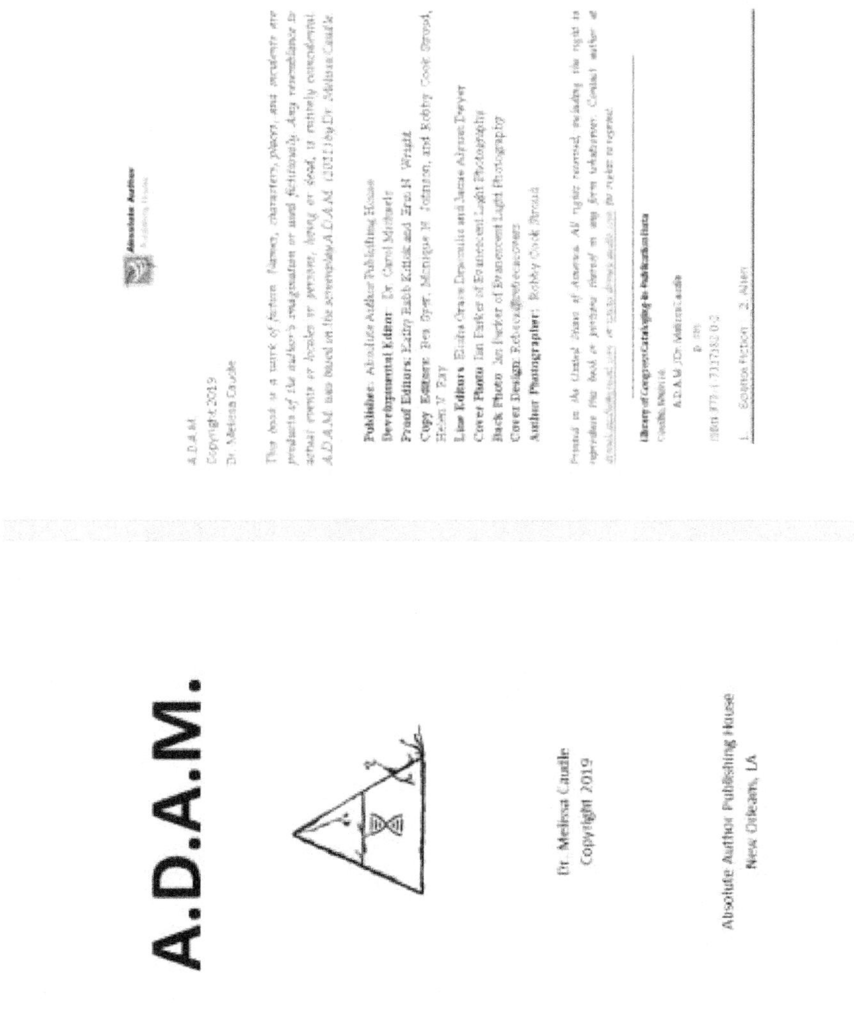

A.D.A.M.

Dr. Melissa Caudle
Copyright 2019

Absolute Author Publishing House
New Orleans, LA

Absolute Author Publishing House

A.D.A.M.
Copyright 2019
Dr. Melissa Caudle

This book is a work of fiction. Names, characters, places, and incidents are products of the author's imagination or used fictitiously. Any resemblance to actual events or locales or persons, living or dead, is entirely coincidental. A.D.A.M. was based on the screenplay A.D.A.M. (2011) by Dr. Melissa Caudle.

Publisher: Absolute Author Publishing House
Developmental Editor: Dr. Carol Michaels
Proof Editors: Kathy Rabb Kittok and Erin N. Wright
Copy Editors: Bea Dyer, Monique N. Johnson, and Robby Cook Stroud, Helen V. Ray
Line Editors: Elisha Grace Desmulis and Jamie Alyson Dwyer
Cover Photo: Ian Parker of Evanescent Light Photography
Back Photo: Ian Parker of Evanescent Light Photography
Cover Design: Rebecca@rebecacovers
Author Photographer: Robby Cook Stroud

Printed in the United States of America. All rights reserved, including the right to reproduce this book or portions thereof in any form whatsoever. Contact author at [illegible] or [illegible] for rights to reprint.

Library of Congress Cataloging-in-Publication Data
Caudle, Melissa
A.D.A.M. / Dr. Melissa Caudle
p. cm.
ISBN 978-1-7337382-0-2
1. Science Fiction 2. Alien

Sample Header and Footer and Chapter Heading

Sample Table of Contents

Contents

The Pitfalls When an Author Converts a Book to an eBook Kindle Format

Write. Edit. Publish. Distribute. The process every published author goes through. Sounds simple enough, but in reality, that four-step process could take months to years for an author to complete. One problem with this four-step formula is that authors think as writers, not publishers. Nowadays, authors must think like publishers because there are so many books available for about every topic in the world. For your book to sell, it must meet publishing standards. It isn't enough for an author to only write, publish their paperback, and then publish their eBook by uploading straight to Kindle Direct Publishing (KDP). There is so much that goes into formatting; so, why would you skimp in formatting your Kindle eBook? Don't you want it perfect like your paperback? You hire editors, cover designers, and sometimes you hire someone to market your book. Why wouldn't you hire a professional Kindle eBook company to format your manuscript? Don't you want the best eBook possible?

TAKE CONTROL TO AVOID THE PITFALLS OF PUBLISHING

When an author attempts to format their eBook for Kindle Direct Publishing, several pitfalls happen to a manuscript — you stand the chance of:

- Not embedding the proper chapter tags,
- Not creating a clickable table of contents,
- Not embedding sections,
- Not embedding proper page breaks,
- Not having your images equally proportioned,
- Not embedding links in the front and back matter, and
- Not having your eBook compatible with all eReaders.

Then, when the author uploads the file to KDP, they get error messages, and the formatting interior is jumbled. It becomes a vicious circle as you attempt to fix the issue only to cause another. Frankly, it's a headache. Sometimes, the eBook gets approved, although it is a mess, and when your eBook goes on sale on Amazon, viewers can look inside your book before they buy. But, if it is a jumbled mess, they will pass on your book and move to another, which means you left money on the table. Why would an author risk so much when there is an affordable solution to the eBook Kindle format sorrows?

CHAPTER FIVE

A Word on Disclaimers

First, I must remind you I am not an entertainment attorney; therefore, I cannot offer you legal advice for your disclaimers. It is best to let your publisher or entertainment attorney, who specializes in intellectual property rights, construct it. Also, keep in mind that each genre requires a different disclaimer, so there isn't a one-size-fits-all. I am providing you with samples for different genres for educational purposes only.

Memoir, Autobiography, or Recent History

> *Some names and identifying details have been changed to protect the privacy of individuals. I have tried to recreate events, locales, and conversations from my memories of them. To maintain their anonymity, sometimes, I have changed the names of individuals and places. In addition, I may have changed some identifying characteristics and details, such as physical properties, occupations, and places of residence.*

Work of Fiction – Novels and Short Stories

This is a work of fiction. Names, characters, businesses, places, events, locales, and incidents are the products of the author's imagination or used fictitiously. Any resemblance to actual persons, living or dead, or actual events is purely coincidental.

Advice, How-to, Self-Help, Motivational Books

Although the author and publisher have tried to ensure that the information in this book was correct at press time, the author and publisher do not assume and disclaim any liability to any party for any loss, damage, or disruption caused by errors or omissions, whether such errors or omissions result from negligence, accident, or any other cause. This book is not intended as a substitute for the medical advice of physicians. The reader should regularly consult a physician on matters relating to their health, particularly regarding any symptoms that may require diagnosis or medical attention.

Sports, Training

The information in this book supplements, not replace, proper (name your sport) training. Like any sport involving speed, equipment, balance, and environmental factors, (this sport) poses some inherent risk. The authors and publishers advise readers to take full responsibility for their safety and know their limits. Before practicing the skills described in this book, be sure that your equipment is well maintained, and do not take risks beyond your level of experience, aptitude, training, and comfort level. Always consult with your physician before beginning any training or participating in sports.

Financial Advice

The Content is for informational purposes only. You should not construe any such information or other material as legal, tax, investment, financial, or other advice. Nothing in this book constitutes a solicitation, recommendation, endorsement, or offer by the author or publisher. All Content is general information and does not address the circumstances of any particular individual or entity. Nothing in the book constitutes professional and/or financial advice, nor does any information in the book constitute a comprehensive or complete statement of the matters discussed or the law relating thereto. You alone assume the sole responsibility for evaluating the merits and risks associated with using any information or deciding based on such information or other content. You agree not to hold the author or publisher or its affiliates for any claim for damages arising from any decision you make based on information available to you through this book.

Health, Healing, Alternative Medicine, Diet Books

This book is for educational purposes only and is not intended to substitute for medical advice from a physician or nutritionist. The reader should regularly consult a physician in all matters relating to their health, especially when and if symptoms require a diagnosis or medical attention.

Career Related and or Business Books

The author and publisher are not responsible for the outcome, either failure or success, of a reader who has read this book and applied the contents to their goals.

Therefore, it is for educational purposes only and should not be considered for other purposes.

Religious – Using Scripture

The content of this book is not meant as religious advice and is for educational purposes only. Any statement should not be construed as taking the place of your ability to evaluate religious claims based on a rational evaluation of the evidence. The authors and publisher shall not be held liable or responsible for misunderstanding or misuse. *Scriptures taken from the Holy Bible, New International Version®, NIV®. Copyright © 1973, 1978, 1984, 2011 by Biblica, Inc.™ Used by permission of Zondervan. All rights reserved worldwide.*

CHAPTER SIX

Generating Your Outline

Here comes the fun part. You finally get to start your rough draft. Is there an easy way to generate your book? Afraid not; nothing comes easy. The pitfall I noticed with new authors is they often don't utilize the planning stage to create their manuscript. Often, they sit and start writing, not having a direction for an ending. Believe it or not, this will slow you down in your writing. Depending on the genre of my book, I always outline the book or use my proprietary Beat Sheet to develop my plots and characters. So, what do these consist of, and how do you use them?

Plot Development

For me, there are three ways to develop a plot.

- Use freedom of expression.
- Use a systematic system from a beat sheet or index cards.
- Write a treatment outlying the story and the characters.

I have used all three equally to my advantage for my novels; however, these work well for nonfiction too.

Freedom of Expression

When you write a novel by sitting at your computer and simply start typing anything and everything until you can't go any further, it is called Freedom of Expression writing. In essence, you think on the go as you develop your plot and characters. You might begin with a small concept and have not thought out the three acts. This means you don't have a direction for your novel, and you hope and pray that something good comes of it.

I don't like this style of writing. Why? Often authors end up with a mess on their hands with shallow characters, lack of backstory, and a very weak Act II at minimum. However, I loved Freedom of Expression writing when I first set out to develop my initial concept. I usually end up with a seven-to-ten-page short story document, almost like a treatment. From there, isolate the three acts, then develop the characters, and transpose those thoughts into the Beat Sheet. However, I may initially begin with Freedom of Expression, but I use a systematic approach to develop my plot and characters afterward. I strongly advise this approach, as it helps define and strengthen your writing. Your readers will thank you, no doubt.

Systematic System

Using a Systematic System in writing is as the name implies. An author will follow a "Recipe" to develop the plot and characters. There are many forms of Systematic writing, one of which is using a Beat Sheet. Another, and an old-fashioned but effective way, is writing your plot points onto index cards and arranging them into a linear order that makes sense for the plot and character development. I've used this method many times.

On the opposite end of the Systematic System, many authors are not fans of this approach because they feel like they are boxed into a format and don't have the freedom to divert. I disagree with them because only a writer's imagination boxes a writer in, not a format. This approach allows for divergence. It encourages it because you don't get lost in the plot structure, and you are nudged to be consistent. The end product, a well-constructed screenplay, is the result.

Outline

The outline approach is also old-fashioned and used by almost all writers in their education. Simply remember your English classes and the teacher forcing you to outline a chapter, a poem, or outline a short story. So, this approach isn't new, and if you are hellbent on not using a Beat Sheet, I'd rather have you use an outline.

An outline will do the same thing as a Beat Sheet, but not as specific. You can outline your plot, which provides you direction, but you might overlook the empowering elements that make a book powerful as an author. That is why I don't use that approach.

Outlining in Chronological Order

The chronological outline arranges your story content according to a progression of time. It doesn't matter if you begin your timeline backward or start at the beginning. Again, that is an author's prerogative to tell their story. The outline method can be used for both fiction and nonfiction. To accomplish a chronological outline, you can use the following outline structure. Of course, change it and add where necessary to complete your content.

I. Topic / Title

A. Generate several working titles.

1. ______________________________
2. ______________________________
3. ______________________________

II. Introduction of Your Story

A. Write a timeline, either from the beginning or begin at the end.

1. 1958 – Year Born
2. Parents
3. Significant Events
4. 1959 – Significant Events
5. 1960 – Significant Events

And so forth.

III. Conclusion

A. Summarize your story and what you want others to get out of it.

Using a Beat Sheet

To use a Beat Sheet to develop your plot, determine key points according to the plot characteristics and identify the characters in advance. This doesn't mean you write the entire story structure beforehand. Instead, it means that you design a general idea about your plot before you write it and then structure yourself accordingly within the parameters. Of course, as you write, elements will change as well as the plot.

To get started using the Beat Sheet, please know that this works best for fiction. Each fiction novel contains a four-act structure. Think about the plot having a beginning, middle, resolution, and ending. Therefore, the plot must be planned accordingly.

The following Beat Sheet keeps an author on track and avoids the pitfalls of having a useless second act or not bringing resolution to the story.

BEAT SHEET DEVELOPMENT FORM

BEAT SCENE DESCRIPTOR	BEAT PLOT POINTS
ACT ONE (1/4 of Book) Introduce the plot/characters with opening action description or visual image	1. 2. 3. 4.
Opening situation/Set up	1. 2.
Introduce the Protagonist and his/her motivation	1. 2. 3.
Conflict begins/Catalyst	1.
Conflict develops	1. 2. 3. 4.
ACT TWO (1/2 of Book) Up the Stakes/obstacles presented	1. 2. 3. 4. 5. 6. 7. 8.
Antagonist reacts	1. 2. 3. 4.
The plot thickens/No way out	1. 2. 3. 4. 5. 6.
Hold your breath moment/Anticipation of outcome	1. 2.
ACT THREE (1/4 of Book) Protagonist regains control	1. 2. 3. 4.
Resolution/Climax/Ending	1. 2.
Final Image/Aftermath of living with the outcome	1. 2. 3.

For now, practice filling out the Beat Sheet for either a short story or a novel. If you have already started your book, fill in the blanks. Remember, you aren't married to this document, and it isn't written in stone. The contents can change quickly.

CHAPTER SEVEN

Character Development

Who Do You Think You Are?

During the development stage of your book's characters, I write a small profile for that character before I assign a name. There are six basic types of characters we develop.

- ✓ **Protagonist** – a character who propels the plot and has something to overcome or achieve.
- ✓ **Antagonist** – a character who is the arch-rival and nemesis to the protagonist.
- ✓ **Motivator** – a usually a supporting character who will move the character along in their decision either on purpose or by happenstance.
- ✓ **Supporter** – usually a supporting character who will guide and help the main character no matter what happens.

✓ **Revealer** – usually a supporting character that will give away clues or disclose private information.

To start, write a brief description for each by creating a profile based on the characters:

- Age
- Race
- Sex
- Religion
- Profession
- Physical Attraction
- Personality
- Attributes

This works for both adult and children's characters. With this said, the questionnaire, although designed for fictional characters, can and should be used for real people in a memoir, biography, or autobiography. It is paramount that you understand who you are writing about, even if it is about yourself. So, please, don't skip this phase if you want to develop your nonfiction manuscript fully.

I also developed a Character Questionnaire form to assist me in profiling my characters. In the developmental stage of *The Keystroke Killer*, I answered the following questions about each of the five-character types before I started writing. Then, I used it if I had to create a new character because the plot demands it. The questionnaire is found on the next couple of pages. Immediately following are the completed versions for each of the main and supporting characters for my book, *The Keystroke Killer*.

Absolute Author
Publishing House

CHARACTER QUESTIONNAIRE

NAME OF CHARACTER:______________________________

☐ **Protagonist** ☐ **Antagonist** ☐ **Motivator** ☐ **Supporter** ☐ **Revealer**

BACKGROUND

1. **How old is this character?**
2. **What race is this character?**
3. **Is the character male or female:** ☐ **Male** ☐ **Female**
4. **Describe the religious background.**
5. **What is the character's profession?**
6. **What does this character look like?**
7. **List words to describe this character's personality.**
8. **What are the character's attributes?**

FAMILY

9. What is the character's family background?
10. What relationship does this character have with the following family members?
    Father:
    Mother:
    Brother:
    Sister:
    Other:
11. What type of relationship is this character in? Love? Married? Divorced? Single?

FINANCIAL

12. What was the economic status of this character growing up?
13. What is the economic status of this character now?

POPULARITY

14. Were they popular as a child in school?
15. Are they popular now as an adult?

INTELLIGENCE

16. What is the intelligence level of your character?

SPEECH PATTERN

17. How does your character talk?

SOCIAL NETWORK

18. What type of friends does this character have?

HOBBIES

19. What hobbies does this character have?

STYLE

20. What is this character's style of clothing? Likes or dislikes?

PERSONALITY/CHARACTER

21. What are this character's strengths/weaknesses?
22. What is this character afraid of?
23. How does this character react to stress?
24. What is the mental health condition of this character?
25. What idiosyncrasies, if any, does this character have?

26. **What drives or motivates this character?**
27. **Describe this character's overall demeanor?**
28. **What secret(s) does your character have?**
29. **How does your character react to success and failure?**

The answers from the Character Questionnaire for each character I created for *The Keystroke Killer* are on the next couple of pages. By reviewing these, you will gain an understanding of the characters and, hopefully, learn how to create yours.

TIP 3: Always create interesting characters, who have flaws, something unique about them, and are in conflict, both inner and in relationships. These will help you to drive your plot and dialogue. Search for ways to make them stand out from anyone else. Determine what is intriguing and different about each one. The more creative you become, the more engaged you will become as a writer.

Absolute Author
Publishing House

CHARACTER QUESTIONNAIRE

NAME OF CHARACTER: ***MATTHEW***

x Protagonist ☐ Antagonist ☐ Motivator ☐ Supporter ☐ Revealer

1. **How old is this character?** *Between 29-34*

2. **What race is this character?** Caucasian

3. **Is the character male or female: X Male** ☐ Female

4. **Describe the religious background.** *No religious preference. He lost his faith in God after his sister was murdered. How can he trust God if God allowed his sister to be killed?*

5. **What is the character's profession?** *Police Detective in his sixth year. Not a rookie. He knows what he is doing.*

6. **What does this character look like?** *An attractive man who hasn't taken care of himself very well due to stress in life, e.g., his sister's death. He looks tired and worn because of the stress and the depression.*

7. **List words to describe this character's personality.** *Matthew is more determined than ever to find the killer of his sister. He is driven, motivated, determined, tormented, haunted, and filled with grief. He feels a deep sense of loss and doesn't want to fall to or succumb to failure.*

8. **What are the character's attributes?** *Matthew is aware of his surroundings, alert, committed to finding the killer, over-confident.*

9. **What is the character's family background?** *As far as others are concerned, he is a close-knit family where he feels responsible for being the caretaker. However, all isn't as it appears. Potential conflict in the home with father, either an abusive father or alcoholic. Mother is loving. Sister was born when Matthew was in grade school.*

10. **What relationship does this character have with the following family members?**

    Father: *Probably bitter; hates him; possibly father didn't want Matthew to be a detective.*
    Mother: *A great relationship. He was protective of her from the abuse of his father.*
    Brother: *NONE*
    Sister: *He adored his little sister and was her protector.*
    Other: *Looked up to his grandfather that was the Chief of Police.*

11. **What was the economic status of this character growing up?** *Because of the father's alcohol abuse, he couldn't keep a job. Mother did what she could, holding down two to three jobs as a waitress, housekeeper, and taking in other people's laundry. They got by, but Matthew began working at sixteen to help support his mother and sister. He had to forget about having a normal high school life and wanted better for his* sister.

12. **What is the economic status of this character now?** *Because Matthew worked his way through college, saved where he could, and now has a good-paying job, he makes a decent living. He has a new car and a nice apartment.*

13. **Was your character popular as a child in school?** *Matthew stayed to himself because he was embarrassed by his father and couldn't get involved in extracurricular activities because he felt responsible for helping support the family.*

14. **Are they popular now as an adult?** *Matthew is a great detective and is admired by his peers. He has made it a point to be the good guy.*

15. **What is the intelligence level of your character?** *He is smart and is street-smart, having grown up in the environment he did. He can more than get by with computers and electronics. He is also a good mechanic.*

16. **How does your character talk?** He is methodical and straightforward. He means what he says and says what he means.

17. **What type of friends does this character have?** *Basically, Matthew doesn't have a social life. He turns to his work.*

18. **What hobbies does this character have?** *If Matthew has a hobby, it is sharpshooting and going to the gun range to keep his skills up. He collects guns and assorted weapons.*

19. **What is this character's style of clothing? *Likes or dislikes?*** *Matthew is simplistic. He sticks to the basics of jeans and a colored shirt. Nothing bright or flashy. Clothes are wrinkled, although clean.*

20. **What type of relationship is this character in?** *Matthew has no love life. All of his time is spent in catching the killer of his sister.*

21. **What are this character's strengths?** *Sniper ability, versatile, dedicated, trustworthy, honest, physically fit.*

22. **What are this character's weaknesses?** *Driven by grief, doesn't take time for himself, caught up in a cat-and-mouse game.*

23. **What is this character afraid of?** *Not being able to catch the killer and failing to avenge his sister's murder.*

24. **How does this character react to stress?** *Work stress doesn't bother Matthew. He is quick in his thinking and responds quickly. He can make a decisive decision to bring resolution to stressful situations.*

25. **What is the health condition of this character?** *He is in good health. He eats right and exercises. However, the stress and grief of losing his sister are getting to him.*

26. **What idiosyncrasies, if any, does this character have?** *He has a habit of rolling two bullets between his fingers when he thinks. He loves to smoke.*

27. **What drives this character?** *The death of his sister and to avenge her death.*

28. **Describe this character's overall demeanor?** *Depressed and grief-stricken. He gets along well with his peers and is liked. His happiness has been replaced with grief, and he can't forgive himself for not saving his sister.*

29. **What secret(s) does your character have?** *As others think, he hides the fact that his family isn't the perfect "Leave it to Beaver" family. Instead, he is finding solace by drinking.*

30. **What is your character's pain tolerance? Emotional? Physical?** *He used to handle anything until he was forced to deal with his sister's death. He is in great shape.*

31. **How does your character react to success and failure?** *When Matthew succeeds, he takes pride. When he fails, he faults himself and takes it too personally by not forgiving himself.*

Absolute Author
Publishing House

CHARACTER QUESTIONNAIRE

NAME OF CHARACTER: THE KEYSTROKE KILLER/JUDAS

☐ Protagonist **XAntagonist** ☐ Motivator ☐ Supporter ☐ Revealer

1. **How old is this character?** *Ageless but perceived as older and wiser.*

2. **What race is this character?** *Appears to be multicultural in race, whereas it is difficult to determine his race. Not Caucasian or African American.*

3. **Is the character male or female: X Male** ☐ Female *(Could be androgynous.)*

4. **Describe the religious background.** *None/he or she thinks they are God.*

5. **What is the character's profession?** *None/never stated. He is the one with the control.*

6. **What does this character look like?** *The face of this character is never really seen. Always in the shadows or seen from the back. A mysterious character.*

7. **List words to describe this character's personality.** *He is strong-willed with control and power. Others fear him.*

8. **What are the character's attributes?** *Resourceful, powerful, patient, focused, determined.*

9. **What is the character's family background?** *A loner. Has no family. The world, if not the universe, is his or her creation.*

10. **What relationship does this character have with the following family members?** *No family.*

    Father:
    Mother:
    Brother:
    Sister:
    Other:

11. **What was the economic status of this character growing up?** *There is no economic status to compare.*

12. **What is the economic status of this character now?** *Lives obscured in a moderate living environment. He wants to blend in.*

13. **Were they popular as a child in school?** *No sign of a childhood. He is what he is from the beginning to the end. It's not a popularity contest.*

14. **Are they popular now as an adult?** *It's not a popularity contest. Popularity doesn't apply to them.*

15. **What is the intelligence level of your character?** *Superior intelligence. Possibly the most superior and superhuman in skills and thinking. He is in control.*

16. **How does your character talk?** *He only speaks on one occasion in the end. His voice is to sound direct and trusting as to not to alert Matthew. He blends. There is nothing distinctive about his voice or the way he says things.*

17. **What type of friends does this character have**? *None.*

18. **What hobbies does this character have?** *None.*

19. **What is this character's style of clothing? Likes or dislikes?** *He is only seen in black and ominous attire. Creepy. Think in terms of The Boston Strangler's Trench Coat.*

20. **What type of relationship is this character in? Love? Married? Single?** *NONE*

21. **What are this character's strengths?** *All-powerful and in control. Knows everything and every detail. He has power over others.*

22. **What are this character's weaknesses?** *Because he is so powerful, he doesn't realize his vulnerability.*

23. **What is this character afraid of?** *Nothing.*

24. **How does this character react to stress?** *He never shows emotion. Never smiles, never shows stress.*

25. **What is the health condition of this character?** Poor.

26. **What idiosyncrasies, if any, does this character have?** *He smokes. He walks with a limp as he has taken on a human form.*

27. **What drives this character?** *The power over others and deciding who lives and who dies.*

28. **Describe this character's overall demeanor?** *Forceful and strong. Non-emotional.*

29. **What secret(s) does your character have?** *That he is not part of the human race. He maintains the human race as a game.*

30. **What is your character's pain tolerance? Emotional? Physical?** *He is vulnerable after taking on the human form; therefore, he feels pain. He walks with a limp.*

31. **How does your character react to success and failure?** *He never shows his emotions to either himself or to others.*

Absolute Author
Publishing House

CHARACTER QUESTIONNAIRE

NAME OF CHARACTER: BLAZE

☐ Protagonist ☐ Antagonist **X Motivator** ☐ Supporter ☐ Revealer

1. **How old is this character?** *18-21 years-old*

2. **What race is this character?** *Caucasian*

3. **Is the character male or female:** ☐ Male ***X*** *Female*

4. **Describe the religious background.** *She was raised by a Christian family and believes in God.*

5. **What is the character's profession?** *A college student supported by her loving parents.*

6. **What does this character look like?** *A very attractive female, beautiful smile, long brown hair, thin, and physically fit.*

7. **List words to describe this character's personality.** *Fun, pleasant, giddy, generous, fair, corky in a way.*

8. **What are the character's attributes?** *Smart and dependable.*

9. **What is the character's family background?** *Her parents are wealthy. Mom is a stay-at-home mom and social activist, and country club scene goer. Dad is an excellent provider who works in a white-collar profession. The family is from old money.*

10. **What relationship does this character have with the following family members?**

    Father: *She is Daddy's little girl who has him wrapped around her fingers.*
    Mother: *Looks up to her mom and admires her.*
    Brother: *NONE*
    Sister: *NONE*
    Other: Nanny - *Only Child -- due to inherit wealth of family.*

11. **What was the economic status of this character growing up?** *Wealthy Parents; large mansion.*

12. **What is the economic status of this character now?** *She lives on a stipend. Has own apartment near campus that parents pay for.*

13. **Were they popular as a child in school?** *Extremely. Every girl wanted to be her, and every boy wanted to date her. Homecoming Queen and cheerleader.*

14. **Are they popular now as an adult?** *She is still the center of attention with her friends and in college.*

15. **What is the intelligence level of your character?** *Above average. Although her parents can afford her college, she won the Academic Presidential Scholarship.*

16. **How does your character talk?** *She is southern from New Orleans going to school in New York. Her accent stands out, but she is well-spoken.*

17. **What type of friends does this character have?** *She makes friends easily as she is likable. She gravitates toward others like herself -- upscale with class and brains.*

18. **What hobbies does this character have?** *Golf, photography, writing poetry, and singing.*

19. **What type of relationship is this character in? Love? Married? Single?** *Single and enjoying playing the field. There are plenty of fish in the sea to choose from.*

20. **What are this character's strengths?** *Smart, witty, fun to be with, a great friend.*

21. **What are this character's weaknesses?** *Spoiled. Used to getting what she wants.*

22. **What is this character afraid of?** *Car wrecks, which is why she either rides a bike or walks, fearing becoming crippled like her grandmother, not living up to her parent's expectations.*

23. **How does this character react to stress?** *Poorly. It shows in her behavior with nervousness.*

24. **What is the health condition of this character?** *Great.*

25. **What idiosyncrasies, if any, does this character have?** *She fidgets when nervous. Will twirl her hair or pace the floor.*

26. **What drives this character?** *The need to succeed.*

27. **Describe this character's overall demeanor?** *Pleasant and fun. Smiles a lot.*

28. **What secret(s) does your character have?** *She had a brief affair with one of her teachers in high school.*

29. **What is your character's pain tolerance? Emotional? Physical?** *She doesn't deal with pain very well. Everything needs to be fixed right away. Can endure the physical pain of running five or more miles.*

30. **How does your character react to success and failure?** *She celebrates success; dements in failure.*

Absolute Author
Publishing House

CHARACTER QUESTIONNAIRE

NAME OF CHARACTER: JENNI

☐ Protagonist ☐ Antagonist ☐ Motivator **X Supporter** ☐ Revealer

1. **How old is this character?** *18-21*

2. **What race is this character?** *Caucasian or Asian.*

3. **Is the character male or female:** ☐ Male ***X Female***

4. **Describe the religious background.** *This character identifies with our motivator character and, therefore, shares the same religious belief. Will be Christian.*

5. **What is the character's profession?** *College student; possibly has a part-time job as a waitress or at a clothing store in the mall.*

6. **What does this character look like?** *She is pretty, but not as pretty as the main female lead. Causes boys to look.*

7. **List words to describe this character's personality.** *Fun and outgoing. Will be outspoken.*

8. **What are the character's attributes?** *Smart, witty, trustworthy.*

9. **What is the character's family background?** *Comes from a divorced family, lives with her father.*

10. **What relationship does this character have with the following family members?**

Father: *Great relationship; relies on him for everything.*
Mother: *Tension between the two; mother left the marriage because of another man.*
Brother: *Is protective of little brother.*
Sister: *Best of friends.*
Other:

11. **What was the economic status of this character growing up?** *Her father earns a modest income but isn't wanting. She uses her part-time job to buy clothes to stay up with the trendsetting lead female.*

12. **What is the economic status of this character now?** *Struggles but makes do with what she has.*

13. **Were they popular as a child in school?** *Not one of the most popular, but had lots of friends. Lived in the shadow of an older sister.*

14. **Are they popular now as an adult?** *Remains in her clique, not the sorority-type girl.*

15. **What is the intelligence level of your character?** *Smart, but not a* genius.

16. **How does your character talk?** *Tends to over pronounce words so she can impress others.*

17. **What type of friends does this character have?** *The lead character and a couple of others, both male and female, within her social circle.*

18. **What hobbies does this character have?** *Bowling, modeling.*

19. **What is this character's style of clothing? Likes or dislikes?** *Likes the latest trends and goes retro; doesn't like to wear things twice to parties.*

20. **What type of relationship is this character in? Love? Married? Single?** Interested in one guy since high school.

21. **What are this character's strengths?** *She is street smart, having grown up without a mother and forced to take care of herself while her father worked.*

22. **What are this character's weaknesses?** *Overspends and drinks too much at parties. No self-control.*

23. **What is this character afraid of?** *Of being alone since her mother deserted the family when she was young. Not being loved for who she is.*

24. **How does this character react to stress?** *She drinks.*

25. **What is the mental health condition of this character?** *Has a complex because of the desertion issue with mom.*

26. **What idiosyncrasies, if any, does this character have?** *She twitches her nose. Possible suspect of cocaine use, although never confirmed.*

27. **What drives this character?** *The need to succeed and be something someday. She wants to be better than her mother.*

28. **Describe this character's overall demeanor?** *Happy. Hides problems very well from others.*

29. **What secret(s) does your character have?** *She wants to join the Navy.*

30. **What is your character's pain tolerance? Emotional? Physical?** *She is a strong individual, having to deal with family issues.*

31. **How does your character react to success and failure?** *She thrives on success, such as a "B" on an exam, even if it is small. When she fails, she goes off on a spending spree she can't afford, then regrets it.*

Absolute Author
Publishing House

CHARACTER QUESTIONNAIRE

NAME OF CHARACTER: MAGDALENE "MAG"

ROLE: ☐ Protagonist ☐ Antagonist ☐ Motivator **X Supporter** ☐ Revealer

1. **How old is this character?** *22-24*

2. **What race is this character?** *Any*

3. **Is the character male or female:** ☐ Male *X Female*

4. **Describe the religious background.** *Wasn't raised in the church. Is more agnostic.*

5. **What is the character's profession?** *College student. Works on campus in the library to help pay tuition.*

6. **What does this character look like?** *Pretty/Pageant worthy.*

7. **List words to describe this character's personality.** *Think in terms of a beauty queen outlook. Always knows what to say.*

8. **What are the character's attributes?** *Smart, great body, and piercing eyes.*

9. **What is the character's family background?** *The oldest of seven girls. Is a twin.*

10. **What relationship does this character have with the following family members?**

Father: *Great relationship. She wants to be just like him.*
Mother: *Often jealous because she gets attention. She is a prior Miss U.S.A.*
Brother: *None*
Sister: *Six sisters, including an identical twin.*
Other: None

11. **What was the economic status of this character growing up?** *Upper middle class. Both parents are professionals -- doctor and a teacher.*

12. **What is the economic status of this character now?** *On a scholarship, has enough money but isn't wealthy.*

13. **Were they popular as a child in school?** *Very, a cheerleader.*

14. **Are they popular now as an adult?** *Yes, a cheerleader at college.*

15. **What is the intelligence level of your character?** *Smart; grades are outstanding. She takes pride in As and gets upset if she gets anything but an A. Her grades drive her.*

16. **How does your character talk?** *Very attractive and sexy voice. She commands the room with her voice and presence.*

17. **What type of friends does this character have?** *They are as pretty as she is, as her vanity can get in the way.*

18. **What hobbies does this character have?** *Beauty Pageants; coaching younger girls in pageants.*

19. **What is this character's style of clothing? Likes or dislikes?** *Very modern and classic style. Looks like she is always ready for a photograph. Nothing is ever out of place with her wardrobe, hair, or make-up. Picture perfect at all times.*

20. **What type of relationship is this character in? Love? Married? Single?** *She is not in a relationship.*

21. **What are this character's strengths?** *Her eyes and looks. Sense of style. She is also an encourager to others.*

22. **What are this character's weaknesses?** *She can come across as vain and shallow. Although she isn't shallow, she avoids a true relationship because she was heartbroken once.*

23. **What is this character afraid of?** *Failure to meet expectations, she places on herself. She is driven to succeed.*

24. **How does this character react to stress?** *Goes on an eating binge then regrets it. Will often cry in the dark, holding a teddy bear she has had since she was three years old. Flight vs. fight mentality.*

25. **What is the mental health condition of this character?** *She is strong in character and has a positive outlook on life. The mental attitude of a champion beauty queen.*

26. **What idiosyncrasies, if any, does this character have?** *She is always fixing her friends' clothes. If there is lint on their clothes, she will remove it. She fixes her friend's hair if it is out of place.*

27. **What drives this character?** *The need to succeed and be the center of attention.*

28. **Describe this character's overall demeanor?** *Friendly, supportive, and outgoing.*

29. **What secret(s) does your character have?** *She once had a lesbian experience at a beauty pageant. It was experimental, but she regrets it and doesn't want anyone to know.*

30. **What is your character's pain tolerance? Emotional? Physical?** *Low. She gets upset easily at the smallest things. She lets others know if she isn't feeling well and uses it as an excuse.*

31. **How does your character react to success and failure?** *Celebrates success, goes into hiding with failure.*

Absolute Author
Publishing House

CHARACTER QUESTIONNAIRE

NAME OF CHARACTER: LANDLORD

ROLE: ☐ Protagonist ☐ Antagonist ☐ Motivator ☐ Supporter **X** Revealer

1. **How old is this character?** *50-60*
2. **What race is this character?** *Can be any race, most likely from India.*
3. **Is the character male or female:** ***X*** *Male* ☐ Female (can be either)
4. **Describe the religious background.** *Buddhist.*
5. **What is the character's profession?** *Landlord of apartment dwelling.*
6. **What does this character look like?** *Stereotypical of a landlord.*
7. **List words to describe this character's personality.** *Straightforward and stand-offish.*
8. **What are the character's attributes?** *Knows what he or she is doing. Can close a deal.*
9. **What is the character's family background?** *From a large family who lives in the building.*
10. **What relationship does this character have with the following family members?**

Father: *A controlling father.*
Mother: *Abused by his father.*
Brother: *Uncles and family back in India.*
Sister:
Other:

11. **What was the economic status of this character growing up?** *Poor who came to America to seek the American Dream.*

12. **What is the economic status of this character now?** *Gets by on income from apartment.*

13. **Were they popular as a child in school?** *Unknown.*

14. **Are they popular now as an adult?** *Keeps to himself.*

15. **What is the intelligence level of your character?** *Average.*

16. **How does your character talk?** *Deep accent from India.*

17. **What type of friends does this character have?** *Unknown.*

18. **What hobbies does this character have?** *Unknown.*

19. **What is this character's style of clothing? Likes or dislikes?** *Simplistic.*

20. **What type of relationship is this character in? Love? Married? Single?** *Married and supports a large family.*

21. **What are this character's strengths?** *Can complete a "Honey Do" list.*

22. **What are this character's weaknesses?** *Lack of interpersonal skills.*

23. **What is this character afraid of?** *Not being able to support his family and being deported back to India.*

24. **How does this character react to stress?** *Ulcers. Worries a lot.*

25. **What is the health condition of this character?** *Good health.*

26. **What idiosyncrasies, if any, does this character have?** *Points finger at others while talking.*

27. **What drives this character?** *Money.*

28. **Describe this character's overall demeanor?** *Non-committal. Seems cold and indifferent.*

29. **What secret(s) does your character have?** *He came to America without a Visa as a stowaway on a freight ship.*

30. **What is your character's pain tolerance? Emotional? Physical?** *Above and beyond the call of duty. Strong.*

31. **How does your character react to success and failure?** *Failure isn't an option for him.*

After reading each questionnaire for the characters for *The Keystroke Killer*, do you feel as if you understand them? Do you have an insight into each one and the type of life they may lead? Understanding your characters is vital in developing your story.

The answers for each character during the development stage were not written in blood or on stone. They are intended to be used as a guideline to develop and maintain a character. The answers can and do change as the plot develops. However, they serve as the first backstory creation for each character. A prime example is for the Landlord. In the developmental stage, I wrote him as coming from India. However, by the time I finished writing the novel, the character developed into a fat, gross, bald, overweight bigot.

TIP 4: Keep the questionnaire up to date as your character evolves.

CHAPTER EIGHT

Opening Narrative

You know the saying, "First impressions are lasting impressions," or "You never get a second chance at making a first impression." These are never truer for a book's opening narrative. What is an opening narrative? Simply stated, an opening narrative is a hook that an author uses to grab the reader's attention. The first line of a book presents a character, plot, or environment that sets the stage for the rest of the book. This applies to fiction and nonfiction. There are many famous first lines in books.

> *Mr. Jones, of the Manor Farm, had locked the hen houses for the night but was too drunk to remember to shut the pop-holes.* ***Animal Farm* – George Orwell**

> *Mr. and Mrs. Dursley, of number four, Privet Drive, were proud to say that they were perfectly normal, thank you very much.* ***Harry Potter* – J. K. Rowling**

> *We went to the moon to have fun, but the moon turned out to completely suck.* ***Feed* – *M.T.* Anderson**

> *In an old house in Paris that was covered with vines lived twelve little girls in two straight lines.* ***Madeline*** **– Ludwig Bemelmans**

For many authors, an opening narrative is the most difficult to write and takes many attempts before you get it exactly as you want it. Unfortunately, aspiring authors make the mistake of not revisiting the opening narrative and thus miss a great opportunity to hook their readers. The narrative has several purposes:

- ✓ Creative and engaging opening narratives make the reader want to keep reading. They get hooked immediately into your story.
- ✓ If written effectively, an opening narrative will introduce the book's theme or themes.
- ✓ Opening narratives make bold statements as to what a reader may expect.
- ✓ A strong opening sets the story and plot in motion.
- ✓ Opening narratives also set the tone for the rest of the book.
- ✓ Opening narratives orient the readers to the content.
- ✓ Opening narratives introduce the narrator's voice to the book.

When readers begin your book, they are already interested in it or wouldn't have purchased it. Don't disappoint them by not having a strong opening narrative. It is an author's responsibility to entice the reader so that they want to keep reading. Look at my opening narrative for my book *Never Stop Running.*

1. OPEN THE DOOR

Dr. Grayson sat in a Victorian chair; his eyes focused on Jackie, who lay in a deep hypnotic state on a worn royal blue velvet chaise. The scar that ridged from her scalp to below her cheek covered by makeup embarrassed Jackie as she leaned her face against the pillow to hide it.

"From this point on, when I say sleep and snap my fingers, you will remember this state and go to it. Now breathe in and out." Dr. Grayson drew a deep breath.

Jackie responded to his suggestion with a huge-heaved sigh of relief.

"Jackie, I'm going to ask you a series of questions. You will not awaken but stay in this peaceful state. You will remain aware of your surroundings. Noises won't bother you. You will only respond to my voice. Do you understand?"

"Yes."

"Jackie, search through your past and find a door and enter." Dr. Grayson observed Jackie's body language and eye movement beneath her eyelids, giving her time to select a door. "Do you see the door?"

"I don't know which one to enter."

"The choice is yours. Think of a time in your past and open the door."

Her eyelids fluttered, her facial muscles flattened, and she looked more mannequin than human. Her right index finger lifted. "That one."

Dr. Grayson shook his head in approval. "That's great Jackie, open the door and step through. Where are you?"

"I'm in a scary place. I feel cold. It's really cold… dark… It's misty."

"Nothing can harm you, Jackie; you're safe. What are you doing in this place?"

"I'm in a dark alley."

"Are you alone?"

She barely shook her head. "Someone else is here… He's calling a woman's name."

In his hypnotherapist mind, Dr. Grayson analyzed her statement. "What name?"

"Gertrude."

"What is Gertrude doing?"

∞

Gertrude, age twenty-three, dressed in an 1880s overcoat with a silver-fox fur collar and an 1880s hat, ran down a dark alley lit only by the orange glow of the oil street lamps and the blood moon. Fog graced the area as a light mist sprinkled. She tried to catch her breath. Smoke from the heat of her breath clashed with the cold misty night air.

A large man who wore a black Gothic cape chased her. "Gertrude! Stop! You'll never get away with this."

Gertrude bolted to escape him. She tripped and fell, scraping both knees; the ground ripped her silk stockings. With the man in close pursuit, she pushed herself up and ran. She lengthened her stride as she looked over her shoulder.

Within an arm's-length of her, the man gained ground; he swiftly closed in. He lifted a butcher knife, lunged at her, and pierced her through her back.

Her body lurched forward as she fell in slow motion and landed in a mud puddle face down. The clammy chill of death gripped her.

He kneeled, rolled her over, and jerked her brass crystal domed watch pendant from around her neck. She heaved as she took her last breath.

∞

Jackie raised her hips, wiggled her shoulders, and exhaled.

"Relax, Jackie, he can't harm you; you're safe."

Jackie jolted. "He killed Gertrude; I saw him kill her." Jackie heavily breathed as her heart pounded against her ribcage.

"Jackie, what year did Gertrude die?"

"October eleventh, eighteen seventy-nine."

He pondered the date. "All right, Jackie, let's move somewhere else. I want you to think of a calm, peaceful place, a beautiful place."

Jackie bolted up with her eyes wide opened. She put her hand on her forehead and heaved. "I don't want to do this."

"Please know you made extreme progress."

"I'm finished for today; I want to go home."

"Jackie, remember your subconscious has a way to deal with your fears if you allow it."

Jackie's voice cracked as emotions flowed. "It's just overwhelming." Jackie cleared her throat and held back her tears.

"I understand. Sometimes when we witness past events, we can become confused and scared. This is a normal process."

"I don't understand what just happened." A tear rolled down her mascara-smeared-scarred face. "Who did I see die?"

Did the above excerpt grab your attention? Did I hook you into wanting to read more? Do you know the theme after reading the opening? What bold statement did I present in the opening? Do you have a clue what to expect because I set the plot in motion? Can you tell the narrator's voice?

Reading the opening narrative makes it easy for the reader to ascertain that the main character is Jackie, and the supporting character is Dr. Grayson. They have a professional relationship as he is her hypnotherapist. I bring in the book's tone by setting up the first regression session where a past life is revealed, setting the structure and theme. It also ends in a cliffhanger, with Jackie asking, "Who did I just see die?" Of course, as an author, I don't have to point out these things, as a well-written opening will do all that for the reader.

A Strong and Powerful Opening

Now read the excerpt below. This is the same opening narrative, without the power behind it.

1. OPEN THE DOOR

Dr. Grayson looked at Jackie, who was in a deep hypnotic state. The scar below her cheek leaned against the pillow.

"From this point on, when I say sleep and snap my fingers, you will remember this state and go to it. Now breathe in and out. Jackie, I'm going to ask you a series of questions. You will not awaken but stay in this peaceful state. You will remain aware of your surroundings. Noises won't bother you. You will only respond to my voice. Do you understand?"

"Yes."

"Jackie, search through your past and find a door and enter. Do you see the door?"

"I don't know which one to enter."

"The choice is yours. Think of a time in your past and open the door."

Her right index finger lifted. "That one."

That's great Jackie, open the door and step through. "Where are you?"

"I'm in a scary place. I feel cold. It's really cold… dark… It's misty."

"Nothing can harm you, Jackie; you're safe. What are you doing in this place?"

"I'm in a dark alley."

"Are you alone?"

Someone else is here… "He's calling a woman's name."

"What name?"

"Gertrude."

"What is Gertrude doing?"

∞

Gertrude, age twenty-three, ran down a dark alley lit only by the oil street lamps and the moon. A large man who wore a black Gothic cape chased her. "Gertrude! Stop! You'll never get away with this."

Gertrude tripped scraping both knees.

Within an arm's-length of her, the man lunged at her pointing a knife, and pierced her through her back. She fell in slow motion and landed in a mud puddle face down.

He kneeled, rolled her over, and jerked her brass crystal domed watch pendant from around her neck. She took her last breath.

∞

Jackie exhaled.

"Relax, Jackie, he can't harm you; you're safe."

"He killed Gertrude; I saw him kill her."

"Jackie, what year did Gertrude die?"

"October eleventh, eighteen seventy-nine."

"All right, Jackie, let's move somewhere else. I want you to think of a calm, peaceful place, a beautiful place."

"I don't want to do this."

"Please know you made extreme progress."

"I'm finished for today; I want to go home."

"Jackie, remember your subconscious has a way to deal with your fears if you allow it."

"It's just overwhelming." Jackie cleared her throat and held back her tears.

"I understand. Sometimes when we witness past events, we can become confused and scared. This is a normal process."

"I don't understand what just happened."
"Who did I see die?"

Did you recognize the difference? What is missing from the above opening narrative is the embellishing that paints a picture in the reader's mind to draw them into the environment, tone, and tension. It takes practice, practice, and more practice to get your opening narrative spot on. There are five types of opening narratives.

- **The Tantalizer** - Openings that begin with a bold statement or moral dilemma. For example, the opening line in Charles Dickens' *A Tale of Two Cities* presents extreme contrasts.

  > *It was the best of times, it was the worst of times, it was the age of wisdom, it was the age of foolishness, it was the epoch of belief....*

- **The Memoir Maker** - Opening narratives that start using "I" and talking about themselves fall into the memoir maker category. For instance, from Michelle Obama's autobiography, *Becoming.*

  > *I spent much of my childhood listening to the sound of striving. It came in the form of bad music....*

- **The Chatter** - Opening narratives beginning with dialogue as in *Charlette's Web* by E. B. White.

  > *"Where's Papa going with that ax?" said Fern to her mother as they were setting the table for breakfast.*

- **The Emcee** - Opening narratives using a narrator or third person to tell the story, such as *The Restaurant at the End of the Universe* by Douglas Adams.

  > *The story so far. In the beginning the Universe was created. This had made a lot of people very angry and been widely regarded as a bad move....*

- **The Set Stager** - Opening narratives that set the stage for everything else. One of the best examples is from the book *The Great Gatsby* by F. Scott Fitzgerald.

  > *In my younger and more vulnerable years my father gave me some advice that I've been turning over in my mind ever since.*

I suggest the following hints to help you craft yours.

State Your Theme

When writing your opening narrative, keep in mind that it should quickly provide the theme of your book without throwing it into a reader's face. One of the best examples is from the book *Anna Karenina* by Leo Tolstoy. The first line, "Happy families are all alike; every unhappy family is unhappy in its own way," sets a world instantly by pointing out dysfunctional families. It encapsulates the differences between happy families and those which are dysfunctional. If you reread the opening of *Never Stop Running,* I quickly identify the themes of hypnosis and reincarnation and present how regression flashbacks will work. This method prepares the reader for what is to follow.

Let a Bizarre or Peculiar Detail Wow Readers

How strange is bizarre? That's the beauty of writing. You can get as strange as you desire. In my opening for *Never Stop Running*, I divulge a strange fact about Jackie: a scar is ridging down her face. Okay, as a stand-alone, that isn't much to go on. However, it raises the question, how did it get there? So, with imagery, I am leading the reader to the moment of how and why Jackie has a scar.

Now consider George Orwell's *1984's* first line, "It was a bright cold day in April, and the clocks were striking thirteen." He has a powerful opening by presenting a strange detail -- the clocks striking thirteen. What world has a clock that has thirteen hours? None, except in fiction. Orwell's usage sets the stage for the strange world and environment the book takes place.

Present Character's Voice

When a writer lets you inside a character's voice in the opening, it gives way to that character's emotions, attitudes, and demeanor. For example, look at the opening from my newest novel, *Secret Romances: A Forbidden Thirst for Love.*

> "I completely take that as a compliment, Dad. Your faith in me is what I always wanted." Angela Arceneaux rolled her eyes as she continued pressing the cell phone against her ear. "The magazine hasn't fallen apart, and it's only been four days since you turned it over to me."

What can you assess about Angela through my opening narrative? What do you know about her after reading the first three sentences?

- ✓ The character's name is Angela.

- ✓ She has daddy issues.
- ✓ She doesn't seem to get the recognition she deserves from her dad.
- ✓ She is in charge of a magazine that her dad handed over to her.

All of this was made evident in the opening narrative. You can also determine Angela's voice as a strong woman ready to take on the world and prove she has what it takes to her dad.

Present the Stakes

When you present the stakes in your opening narrative, it creates automatic tension and lets the reader know the protagonist faces danger. Here is the opening narrative from my book, *The Keystroke Killer: Transcendence*. Read it carefully and see if you can figure out the stakes for my protagonist, Matthew.

CHAPTER 1
The Day of Reckoning

Sunrise

The golden sun peaked from the dark cloudless sky above the city that care forgot. Five fighter jets flew in a disciplined duck formation usually seen at an air show. Less than three feet apart, the synchronize advance provided the aerodynamic advantage as they approached the city known for Mardi Gras and the birthplace of jazz. One inch off the maneuver would be disastrous.

Hipshot, the right wingman spotted the Greater New Orleans Bridge and the murky brown Mississippi River below. "We're making our approach."

"Roger that." Skeeter, the attractive second lieutenant to his left wing flashed a grin of male satisfaction.

"Doesn't look like the bridge is backed up."

The striking commander, James Dylan Taylor, tapped his microphone attached to his pilot's helmet. "Cut the chatter." He flew over the Crescent City hundreds of times and needed no reminder of his location and didn't want to listen to a morning traffic report. His expression covered by his pilot's helmet.

The fly-by non-approved flight over the Mississippi River Bridge to commemorate the death of Livia Lynn Raymond, daughter of the New Orleans Police Commissioner, zoomed close to Mach one. As the air squadron flew over, an old green Ford Taurus driven by Matthew Raymond, Jr. merged into the flow of the morning commute headed west below. As he drove, he listened to the song *New Orleans* by Stevie Nicks.

Matthew's blistering bloodshot green eyes, his crow's feet and dark circles reflected into the rearview mirror which revealed the anguish behind them and made the thirty-year-old look older. His third-day unshaven face, his tossed brown hair, his wrinkled shirt, and faded Levi jeans acknowledged his unkempt style. He made no excuse for his appearance or his depressed demeanor as his eyes fixated ahead at the traffic. *Today is the day I dread the most. It will happen again, and again. It can't be stopped until I die. I could have stopped this in the first place. Livia told me she was in danger.*

His sister's last words haunted him. "Matthew, I'm scared. Somebody is after me." He tried to shake the disturbing message, but the echoes wouldn't stop.

"Somebody is after me. Do something."

In the above excerpt, you are introduced to Matthew, the protagonist. He's troubled and on a mission and dreads this day most each year. The reader is guided into his troubled thoughts after I present the stakes.

Set the Scene

With each opening narrative, the scene should be set. Where does the narrative take place? What city? What country? What year? Off-world? The opportunity is endless. The point is to set it and present it. If you refer to the opening narrative for *The Keystroke Killer: Transcendence*, it is easy to identify that this story is taking place in New Orleans, Louisiana. That doesn't mean you have to state the city, just the scene. Consider the opening narrative for the book *Mutiny on the Bounty* by Charles Nordhoff and James Norman Hall.

> *The British are frequently criticized by other nations for their dislike of change, and indeed we love England for those aspects of nature and life which change the least.*

From the beginning, a reader is transported to England; the scene was set as well as the location.

CHAPTER NINE

WORDINESS

Wordiness? Why the heck would I start this chapter with that word? Believe it or not, many authors make the mistake of trying to add too many words into what they write. Somehow, they feel that more is better, whereas it can have the opposite effect. Every word you use should have meaning and assist in either developing your plot, subplots, or characters. Simply adding fluff doesn't make you a talented writer. Padding a manuscript is a dead giveaway for an amateur writer. As an author, I know the power of words. However, if too wordy, the manuscript becomes cumbersome. Also, when you use too many words, redundancy happens.

You can avoid wordiness and redundancy by carefully examining your manuscript, eliminating unnecessary words and phrases, and omitting unnecessary verbs such as, is, are, was, were, and using an active voice when writing. The goal is for writers to communicate clearly. Here are guidelines to follow to avoid wordiness and redundancy in your manuscript.

Use Key Nouns

Nouns are the subject of your sentence and need to be the focus of each sentence. That is what makes them a key noun.

> **Example:** Beth's essay was an attempt to discredit her professor.

In the above, we know Beth is our subject and that she's trying to discredit her professor. This sentence is wordy and bulky because the subject, Beth, was not used in the key position. Construct the sentence with Beth as the key noun to make this cleaner and less bulky.

> **Revision:** Beth attempted to discredit her professor in her essay.

Use Active Voice

Active voice means that a sentence has a subject that acts upon its verb. **Passive voice** means that a subject receives a verb's action. You may have learned that the passive voice is weak and incorrect, but it isn't that simple. When used correctly and in moderation, the passive voice is fine.

In English grammar, verbs have five properties: voice, mood, tense, person, and number; here, we are concerned with voice. The two grammatical voices are **active** and **passive**.

When the subject of a sentence performs the verb's action, we say that the sentence is in the **active voice**. Sentences in the active voice have a strong, direct, and clear tone. Here are some short and straightforward examples of active voice.

Monkeys adore bananas.

The cashier counted the money.

The dog chased the squirrel.

All three sentences have a basic active voice construction: subject (key noun), verb, and object.

The subject ***monkey*** performs the action described by ***adore***.

The subject, ***the cashier,*** performs the action described by ***counted***.

The subject, ***the dog,*** performs the action described by ***chased***.

Passive Voice

One of the biggest issues I encounter as an editor is authors who write in a passive voice. When authors choose to write in a passive voice, it tells your readers two things about you as a writer. First, you are not polished. Why? To write in passive voice is what I call the easy way out. Anyone can use 'was' or 'were' followed by a weak 'ing' verb. Secondly, writing in this manner, your subject is acted upon rather than doing the action, which weakens your writing. Consider this example.

The family **was going** to Disneyland for Christmas.

The above example is written passively. If you review your writing and use the word search tool in Microsoft Word and search for the word 'was,' you will find many of your passive voice sentences. To modify and enhance your writing, omit the word 'was' and change it to past tense and replace the weak 'ing' verb with a strong verb.

Now consider the rewrite.

The family **traveled** to Disneyland for Christmas.

In the above sentence, I made the subject, family, perform the action -- traveled. I also used a stronger verb, traveled, instead of went. It is a stronger sentence this way. Most passive voice sentences use the forms of **to be**.

- Infinitive – to be
- Present – am, is, are
- Past – was, were
- Present Participle – been
- Present Subjunctive – be
- Past Participle – been
- Past Subjective – were
- Imperative - be

A sentence is passive when the verb acts on the subject. **The passive voice is always constructed with a conjugated form of *to***

***be* plus the verb's past participle**. Doing this usually generates a preposition as well. That sounds much more complicated than it is -- passive voice is relatively easy to detect. For examples of passive voice, we will transform the three active sentences above to illustrate the difference.

Bananas **are** adored by monkeys.

The money **was** counted by the cashier.

The squirrel **was** chased by the dog.

Let's take a closer look at the sentences referring to the monkeys.

Passive Voice: Bananas are adored by monkeys.

Active Voice: Monkeys adore bananas.

The active sentence consists of ***monkeys*** (subject) + ***adore*** (verb) + ***bananas*** (object). The passive sentence consists of ***bananas*** (object) + ***are adored*** (a form of ***to be*** plus the past participle ***adored***) + ***by*** (preposition) + ***monkeys*** (subject). Making the sentence passive flipped the structure and necessitated the preposition ***by***. So, a general rule to avoid passive voice is to do a word search in your document for the word **by**. Never end the sentence with the word "by" following the subject. When you find the word **by**, determine if the sentence's subject follows.

To write actively, use subject, verb, and object in that order.

Passive Voice - Bananas are adored by monkeys.
Active Voice - Monkeys adore bananas.

Passive Voice - The money was counted by the cashier.
Active Voice - The cashier counted the money.

Passive Voice - The squirrel was chased by the dog.

Active Voice - The dog chased the squirrel.

In the examples above, the proper way starts with the subject, the verb, and the object in each case. However, to avoid writing in passive voice requires tons of practice. First, go through your manuscript and identify the sentences written in passive voice and modify them.

Hint: Some editing software, such as Grammarly and ProWritingAid, will identify the passive voice sentences. When you find those, make the necessary changes.

To eliminate passive voice, you must write to make the subject perform the action. Again, make sure your subject comes before the verb.

You can shift the sentence's focus from direct or indirect to the subject. For example, you can transform the following sentences from passive to active voice by removing the form of 'be' to a strong action verb. I have used bold font to identify the passive voice and the weak verbs and, in the revised sentence, marked the stronger verbs and active voice in italics.

Passive: The child **was running** down the hall to **get** to class on time.

Active: The child ***bolted*** through the hall to ***arrive*** to class on time.

Passive Voice: After class, Mary **was starving**, so she **went** to the closest store to **buy** junk food.

Active: After class, Mary's stomach ***growled***, so she ***strode*** to the closest store ***to purchase*** junk food.

Avoid Unnecessary Words

Authors don't realize how many unnecessary words they use. For instance, the following are the most often unnecessary phrases/words used:

- Due to the fact
- In fact
- In the event of
- This shows that
- This serves as a way to
- This is an example of
- Because of the fact
- In order to
- Whether or not
- Depends on certain things
- In my opinion

Look at the following examples and the revisions where I removed the unnecessary and cumbersome words.

Example: Due to the fact that it is January, it will likely snow.

Revision: In January, it will likely snow.

Example: In the event of rain, the wedding will be moved to the atrium.

Revision: If it rains, the wedding will be moved to the atrium.

Example: When an employee gives an award, it shows that they care about the morale of the company.

Revision: When an employer gives an award, they care about the employee's morale.

Example: In order to prepare for surgery, the patient must fast the day before.

Revision: To prepare for surgery, the patient must fast the day before.

Example: The forecaster doesn't know whether or not it will rain tomorrow.

Revision: The forecaster doesn't know whether it will rain tomorrow.

Avoid Words with the Same Meaning

A huge mistake for authors is to pad their sentences with words that have the same meaning. Unfortunately, this creates a stumbling block for the reader, and often they become frustrated. Refer to the examples below:

Example: Dr. Mary Caudle, a physician, is in the process of training a new intern to become a doctor.

Revision: Dr. Mary Caudle is training a new intern.

In this example, there are simply too many modifiers bulking this sentence. First, we know Mary is a physician with the title of Dr. in front of her name, so the modifier following isn't necessary. Likewise, since Dr. Caudle is a physician and is training an intern, what else would they be training them to become? Therefore, the revision is cleaner and less bulky. Finally, it isn't necessary to define Dr. Caudle's occupation twice, as it makes it redundant.

Author's will also become redundant when trying to describe a person. Consider the following:

Example: Dr. Melissa Caudle is a professional editor. She earned a Ph.D. and works as the Senior Editor for Absolute Author Publishing House in New Orleans, Louisiana.

Revision: Melissa Caudle, Ph.D., a professional editor, works for Absolute Author Publishing House in New Orleans, Louisiana.

In this example, I combined the two sentences and deleted the redundancy. I don't need both the Dr. title in front of my name and that I earned a Ph.D. in the sentence.

Also, creating a cumbersome manuscript and redundancy is when an author uses expressions. The most misused include:

Redundant: Twelve midnight, twelve noon
Revisions Midnight, noon

Redundant: In the morning at six a.m.
Revision: At six a.m.

Redundant: In close proximity
Revision: Proximity

Redundant: Each and every
Revision: Each

Redundant: Exactly the same
Revision: Exactly

Redundant: Consensus of opinion
Revision: Consensus

Redundant: I am in the understanding that
Revision: I understand

Redundant: To summarize the above
Revision: In summary

Redundant: One and the same
Revision: The same

Redundant: Period of seven days.
Revision: Seven days, or one week

Redundant: Personally, I believe
Revision: I believe

Redundant: Personally, I think
Revision: I think

Redundant: Absolutely complete
Revision: Complete

Redundant: Assembled together
Revision: Assembled

Redundant: Continue on
Revision: Continue

Redundant: Cooperate together
Revision: Cooperate

Redundant: Still remains
Revision: Remains

Redundant: The reason is because
Revision: Because

Redundant: Concerning the matter of
Revision: About

Redundant: During the course of
Revision: During

Redundant: Regardless of the fact that
Revision: Although

Redundant: Due to the fact that
Revision: Because

Redundant: It is often the case that
Revision: Often

Use Strong Verbs to Express Action Rather Than Nouns

I can't relay how many times I have to change nouns used as verbs when editing. When nouns are formed from verbs, it is called nominalizations, and most will end in -ence, -ness, or -tion.

Example: Today's teenagers need **modification** of its moral values.

Revision: Today's teenagers need to **modify** its moral values.

Don't Use a String of Prepositional Phrases

A prepositional phrase is a modifying phrase consisting of a preposition and its object and can easily be recognized. Prepositional phrases usually start with the words by, for, in, on, out, in, and at. However, combining more than one preposition creates a bulky string, and it is best to avoid the usage. Here are the top prepositional phrases to avoid in your manuscript.

Without a doubt
Without a break
To the best of
To the detriment of
Out of breath
Out of context
To the exclusion of
At a moment's notice
At a price
For a good cause
For the benefit of
For a reason
For a good cause
For the sake of
At face value
Without a hitch
For certain
To one's dismay
To one's credit
To date
Under repair
On the way to
For the fear of
Out of breath
Out of context
Without a delay

At the end of
At an advantage
At the hands of
At the latest
At this juncture
At a speed of
At the front of
At the beginning
In the beginning
At the age of
At the mercy of
At one's discretion
At face value
On the condition of
On a spree
On the way to
On the hour
By all means
By my request
By all accounts

CHAPTER TEN

Enhancing Dialogue

As an author, you spend years honing your craft to write complete sentences error-free and naturally flow. Although it is important that an author write clear sentences and use correct punctuation, that is only half the battle. For most novelists, we have it down pat when writing descriptions and setting the tone, but we have to work at writing authentic dialogue and is far from the on-the-nose dialogue it can get. It's difficult, but it is something as a novelist we must master.

On the Nose Dialogue

When writing dialogue, it is important to remember that when people converse, it is not straightforward. Often, those who converse have hidden agendas, and they hide the truth; they say one thing and mean another; they tell lies; they exaggerate, and so forth. This is far from straightforward dialogue; so, why would a novelist do that to their characters? A character's dialogue must contain more than just words. Sometimes it isn't what they say but what they do with their hands, mouth, eyes, and body language. Read the following short dialogue.

Sample Dialogue

Marge chopped onions as she wiped her tears.

Frank entered; a scowl creased his brow. “What’s wrong, honey?”

“Nothing at all.”

“Then why the tears?”

“Nothing. It’s the onions.”

After reading this brief conversation, we know three things: Marge is cutting onions, her eyes are teary, and Frank wants to know why. She responds, “Nothing at all.” My question to you is, does she mean it? Of course not; there is something else wrong, or is there? If we leave it as is, the reader doesn’t know; they can only surmise.

As a writer, I wouldn't leave this brief dialogue like this; I want to let the reader into the lives of Marge and Frank. I would enhance it with subtexts or add her thoughts, body language, and inner dialogue to draw in the reader. I would do the same thing with Frank. An important thing to remember is that every scene in your book and every paragraph has three parts -- a beginning, middle, and an end. Also, conflict needs to exist. Why? It keeps your readers interested, and if you don't, your dialogue falls flat. Now read the same brief dialogue enhanced with subtext, e.g., emotions, body language, thoughts, etc.

Enhanced Dialogue

Marge chopped onions as she wiped her tears. *If he thinks I'm going to play nice, he has another thing coming.* She sniffled as she gasped, and then lowered her head. Her heart thrummed against her ribcage.

Frank staggered into the kitchen; a scowl creased his brow. “What’s wrong, honey?” His mumbled tone, soft and comforting, grated her nerves.

“Nothing at all.” Marge pursed her lips. She felt her blood pulse in her wrists as she slammed the knife into the onion.

“Then why the tears?” He placed his hand on her shoulder as he planted a gentle kiss on her cheek.

She recoiled and averted his gaze. “Nothing. It’s the onions.” Her sarcastic tone spoke the truth to her words. She jabbed the knife into the bamboo cutting board.

Frank’s eyes widened as he stepped backward. His jaw clenched as a pit formed in his stomach. *Here we go again. I can’t even try to be nice.*

Now that I've added inner thoughts, emotions, body language, etc., the reader has a better idea of the relationship between Marge and Frank, and I added conflict; things aren't hunky-dory in their world. Let's examine the subtext in terms of:

- Body Language
- Visceral Reactions
- Inner Thoughts
- Voice Tone

Body Language

In the following dialogue, I have used body language for both Marge and Frank and bolded them, which indicates their true feelings. It wasn't what they said; it was what their body did.

> Marge chopped onions as she **wiped her tears**. *If he thinks I'm going to play nice, he has another thing coming.* She **sniffled** as **she gasped** and then **lowered her head**. Her heart thrummed against her ribcage.
>
> Frank **staggered** into the kitchen; a **scowl creased his brow**. "What's wrong, honey?" His tone, soft and comforting, grated her nerves.
>
> "Nothing at all." Marge **pursed her lips**. She felt her blood pulse in her wrists as she **slammed the knife** onto the onion.
>
> "Then why the tears?" **He placed his hand on her shoulder** as **he planted a gentle kiss** on her cheek.

She recoiled and **averted his gaze**. "Nothing. It's the onions." Her sarcastic tone spoke the truth to her words. She **jabbed the knife** into the bamboo cutting board.

Frank's **eyes widened** as **he stepped backward.** His **jaw clenched** as a **pit formed in his stomach**. *Here we go again. I can't even try to be nice.*

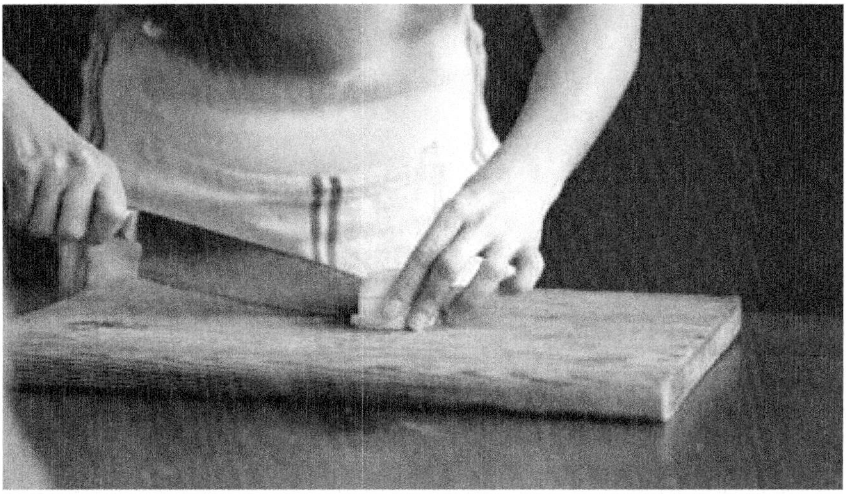

Notice that the body action or body language provided the reader with important information. With these actions, it is easy to tell that something is wrong. We get the idea that she is upset and angry with Frank. She is crying, her blood pressure is raised, and she is angry when she slams the knife. Notice, I never said in the narrative that Marge was angry. I showed her emotion rather than tell you, which is another key to powerful writing. We get a clue that Frank may be drunk, e.g., he staggered, and he might feel guilty, or he is trying to make it up to her. He could also have symptoms of a stroke. As he steps backward and clenches his jaw, he becomes offended by her actions. This brings the reader into their world, emotions, and communication tone.

Visceral Reactions

Visceral reactions are those things that aren't visible. They occur on the inside of a body to explain an emotion or a physical condition. Look at the dialogue again with the visceral reactions in bold print.

> Marge chopped onions as she wiped her tears. *If he thinks I'm going to play nice, he has another thing coming.* She sniffled as she gasped and then lowered her head. Her **heart thrummed against her ribcage**.
>
> Frank staggered into the kitchen; a scowl creased his brow. "What's wrong, honey?" His tone, soft and comforting, **grated her nerves**.
>
> "Nothing at all." Marge pursed her lips. She **felt her blood pulse in her wrists** as she slammed the knife onto the onion.
>
> "Then why the tears?" He placed his hand on her shoulder as he planted a gentle kiss on her cheek.
>
> She recoiled and averted his gaze. "Nothing. It's the onions." Her sarcastic tone spoke the truth to her words. She jabbed the knife into the bamboo cutting board.
>
> Frank's eyes widened as he stepped backward. His jaw clenched as **a pit formed in his stomach.** *Here we go again. I can't even try to be nice.*

In the above example, the reader feels tension because of the visceral reactions. For example, Marge's blood pressure raised, and he felt guilt.

Inner Thoughts

I love inner thoughts because a reader gets inside a character's head, which the other characters don't hear. Using inner thoughts gives readers a sense of knowing something. Look at the dialogue again with the inner thoughts in bold print.

> Marge chopped onions as she wiped her tears. ***If he thinks I'm going to play nice, he has another thing coming.*** She sniffled as she gasped and then lowered her head.
>
> Frank staggered into the kitchen; a scowl creased his brow. "What's wrong, honey?" His tone, soft and comforting, grated her nerves.
>
> "Nothing at all." Marge pursed her lips. She felt her blood pulse in her wrists as she slammed the knife onto the onion.
>
> "Then why the tears?" He placed his hand on her shoulder as he planted a gentle kiss on her cheek.
>
> She recoiled and averted his gaze. "Nothing. It's the onions." Her sarcastic tone spoke the truth to her words. She jabbed the knife into the bamboo cutting board.
>
> Frank's eyes widened as he stepped backward. His jaw clenched as a pit formed in his stomach. ***Here we go again. I can't even try to be nice.***

As a reader, a character's inner thoughts provide a sense of knowing -- an insider's viewpoint. For example, Marge's inner thought tells the reader she is angry without me telling you she's angry. Frank doesn't know it. In Frank's inner thought, the reader learns they fight often, and he may give up on being nice.

Voice Tone

Have you ever played the game, *Say it Ten Times Differently*? Try it. Say, "I hear you," ten different ways. Each time modify your intensity or place accent a different word. The meaning changes. When you write dialogue, the voice tone does this for the reader. Look at the dialogue again with the voice tone in bold print.

Marge chopped onions as she wiped her tears**.** *If he thinks I'm going to play nice, he has another thing coming.* She sniffled as she gasped and then lowered her head. Her heart thrummed against her ribcage.

Frank staggered into the kitchen; a scowl creased his brow. "What's wrong, honey?" **His tone, soft and comforting, grated her nerves.**

"Nothing at all." Marge pursed her lips. She felt her blood pulse in her wrists as she slammed the knife onto the onion.

"Then why the tears?" He placed his hand on her shoulder as he planted a gentle kiss on her cheek.

She recoiled and averted his gaze. "Nothing. It's the onions." **Her sarcastic tone spoke** the truth to her words. She jabbed the knife into the bamboo cutting board.

Frank's eyes widened as he stepped backward. His jaw clenched as a pit formed in his stomach**.** *Here we go again. I can't even try to be nice.*

Now the reader knows exactly how a character's dialogue should be read. Franks sounds apologetic and maybe caring, and Marge, well, she's not being nice or soft-spoken, which changes the entire tone of this dialogue. Their genuine emotions were revealed to the reader by adding a voice tone.

Authentic Dialogue

One major mistake authors make in writing dialogue is the lack of authenticity. Dialogue should be natural as if spoken and not necessarily grammatically correct. Look at this dialogue.

"Get out of my face," Charles pushed his lover away.

"Do not touch me again." Janet's face turned crimson.

"If you would not keep yelling at me, I would not."

"I am finished with you. Get out of my house."

By adding body language, visceral reactions, inner thoughts, and voice tone, this dialogue comes alive onto the page. However, what is missing is authenticity. People talk grammatically correct. Look at the revised dialogue below. I highlighted the fixes.

"Get **outta** my face," Charles pushed his lover away.

"Don't touch me!" Janet's face turned crimson.

"If you **wouldn't** keep on yelling at me, **I wouldn't**."

"**I'm** finished with **you**. Get out of my house."

Master this, and your dialogue will be authentic. For example, it is perfectly fine to use contractions because that's how we speak. Likewise, you can use slang.

Avoid Using Cliches

A cliché is an overused expression that conveys a meaning. It is a way to define a stereotype, but it has negative connotations once used. When you use cliches, it lessens the quality of your writing and demonstrates your lack of creativity and original thoughts. Stay clear of them. Cliches are convenient when writing, show a writer's laziness and don't allow a more profound development of your character. It is critical to innovate and be creative with originality. Readers are distracted and annoyed by them, and, frankly, they do nothing to move your plot forward or to develop your character. Listed below are the main cliches you should avoid.

- Don't use tales from others. Readers want new stories!

- Don't over melodramatize.
- Don't take the lazy way out by using cliches.

Fifty Overused Cliches You Must Avoid

1. All that glitters is gold.
2. To each his own.
3. Take a tiger by the tail.
4. Red as a rose.
5. Avoid it like the Black Plague.
6. Every cloud has a silver lining.
7. Make or break it.
8. Win some, lose some.
9. You can take it or leave it.
10. How time flies when you're having fun.
11. Be there in a jiffy.
12. Head over heels.
13. Don't get your panties in a wad.

14. Kiss and make up.

15. Only time will tell.

16. Scared out of my wits.

17. Scared me to death.

18. At the speed of light.

19. Fly on the wall.

20. Fit as a fiddle.

21. Dead as a doornail.

22. What comes around goes around.

23. Tail between your legs.

24. As old as the hills.

25. The eyes are the way to the soul.

26. A perfect storm.

27. Beating a dead horse.

28. You can bring the horse to water, but you can't make them drink.

29. In the nick of time.

30. Live happily ever after.

31. The grass is greener on the other side.

32. Does the cat have your tongue?

33. Make lemons out of lemonade.

34. What goes around comes around.

35. Karma is a bitch, then you die.

36. Every rose has a thorn.

37. Read between the lines.

38. Read the writing on the wall.

39. Open a can of worms.

40. The apple doesn't fall far from the tree.

41. Calling the kettle black.

42. Ignorance is bliss.

43. Always think outside the box.

44. You soon will get yours.

45. Good things come to those who wait.

46. You're a loose cannon.

47. There's plenty of fish in the sea.

48. Dog day afternoon.

49. Like a kid in a candy store.

50. I got out of the wrong side of the bed.

Ways to Avoid Cliches

To avoid using cliches, consider the following.

1. **Complete the Character Questionnaire provided and intimately know each one**. Ask what words would this character use or never say in a conversation. When you understand your character, the conversation, and dialogue can be adapted to fit. My motto is that a character's dialogue should define them and not the other way around. That is why I avoid using dialogue tags. When a character speaks, a reader should know who is speaking by what they say and not because you wrote, he said, she said. The only way to accomplish this is by understanding your character's personality and relationship with the other person speaking.

2. **Become an active student of listening.** Practice listening to how people talk and say things. That's one reason I am a people observer on cruises. You get a great understanding of how people speak in different regions, countries, and cultures. Then, after you observe enough conversations, you can emulate them in your writing for authenticity.

3. **Use contractions.** When you don't use contractions, your dialogue becomes clumsy, losing authenticity.

4. **Avoid dialogue tags.** Again, using he said, she said, when writing becomes cumbersome and very monotonous for the reader. Research has proven that most readers skip them anyway unless the dialogue is poorly written, and they don't know who is talking. Avoid the cumbersomeness of dialogue tags by using action and emotion that are part of the character's flaws and characteristics.

5. **Listen to your dialogue.** To be a better writer for dialogue, you must listen to it. In Word, you have that ability. Another way is to read your dialogue aloud or have a friend come over and read it with you.

CHAPTER ELEVEN

Describing Action Sequences

Lights! Camera! Action! I know you typically associate this phrase with a movie, so what does it have to do with writing action sequences? Easy. Action propels a plot forward and adds conflict. Like everything we write in a manuscript, it must move the plot forward or develop the character; otherwise, it only takes up space on the page. You must articulate a fight scene to perfection, or it will lose its value. It is imperative that the action sequence, if called for in your plot, be as authentic as your dialogue. The biggest mistake I see is when an author over describes the action sequence. There are seven types of action scenes.

1. **Combat** – These scenes include hand-to-hand combat like in *Raging Bull* and *Star Wars.*

2. **Fights with weapons** – These scenes include all types of weapons hurled at each other or a shootout scene.

3. **Chase** – Many fights start and then escalate into a chase scene.

4. **Use of Superpowers** – I love these scenes, and they speak for themselves in terms of anything goes. However, be mindful of how you construct your scene, so it doesn't become sappy or stereotypical.

5. **Escape** – Often, characters find themselves in predicaments that require them to flee the scene. This is where the conflict in a scene thrives.

6. **Rescue** – A rescue scene can have paramedics rescue someone trapped in a car after a wreck or from a burning building, and a lot more.

7. **Sport's Competition** – There is always action from dribbling a ball down the court to fighting in a rink.

Before you jump into writing a fight scene or action sequence, detail the following to guide you.

1. Ask how this scene fits into the context of the plot and for the characters involved.

2. Where does this sequence take place, and why?

3. What skills do the characters bring with them? This should be included in the Character's Questionnaire you completed in the early development stage. If you didn't, go back and revise to include them.

4. Decide who the reader should be cheering.

So, how do you write an action sequence that is meaningful and impactful?

1. **Act out the scene.** Before you write the first word of an action sequence, act it out. Pay close attention to what you do and how you move. That way, you can clearly describe the action and visceral reactions of the human body. For example, if you write about climbing up a hill, either mimic climbing or climb one. Pay extreme attention to your motions, visceral reactions, and overall feelings. Do you get leg cramps? Do your thighs burn? Do you get out of breath? Or is it easy-going because you run a marathon? The important part is that these reactions must match the character's ability and condition. For example, a marathon runner wouldn't get out of breath quickly, nor would a third-degree Black Belt. However, an elderly woman or out-of-shape teen would.

2. **Observe others' actions.** It is imperative to watch swimmers swim, runners run, boxers box, etc., to write impactful action sequences. You can go to the park and watch runners, attend a swim meet, or attend a boxing match. Take notes of everything you see from what they are wearing, their movements, and things they say. All of this will play into your action sequences.

3. **Keep your descriptions to a minimum.** Only include the action. Avoid overusing adjectives and adverbs. Instead, I advise using short, choppy sentences and even an occasional incomplete sentence.

4. **Minimize dialogue.** Decide if you are writing an action sequence or dialogue. Only rarely should you do both in an

action sequence. The only time I use dialogue in an action sequence is to break it up to give a reader a break. But, again, I only do this sparingly.

5. **Use strong verbs.** I rarely worry about using strong verbs to keep my creativity flowing when writing my first draft. However, during editing, I will change them to strong verbs. The difference between strong verbs and weak verbs is easy. Consider the word run. Boring! Instead, use a thesaurus and find powerful alternative words. Stronger verbs include sprint, race, lope, bolt, dart, dash, jog, scamper, scurry, etc.

6. **Avoid using passive voice.** Again, review the previous information on passive voice and apply it to your action sequence.

7. **Learn by reading screenplays.** When writing a screenplay, screenwriters are mainly concerned with dialogue and action. I advise you to read action screenplays to determine how they write them. You can download plenty of screenplays for this. Look for the kinds of sentences they use, the modifiers, and how the body moves. However, refrain from plagiarizing.

8. **Learn by reading master action writer's books.** Yes, learn from the best. My favorite action writers are Lee Child, John Connolly, Patricia Cornwell, and Mario Puzo. They are true masters of action sequences.

9. **Know the stakes and outcome before you write.** Don't write an action scene for the sake of one. Instead, ask if it is even necessary and what the context of the scene is to move the plot forward. If you can't determine these answers, likely you don't need an action scene. For

instance, consider a car chase scene over a bridge. Who is being chased and why? Is it a robber being chased by the police? Or is it a Ferrari race? Both have implications in your action sequence. The key is to know the stakes and outcome, which levels the playing field and moves the plot forward.

10. **Include urgency.** If the action isn't urgent, why have it? You want to ramp up the scene and get the reader's heart pumping. Writing a boring action sequence won't cut it.

11. **Include barriers.** Don't make it easy for your character to win the fight, race, escape, etc. Rather, provide barriers by creating a no-way-out situation, inclement weather, innocent bystanders in the way, etc. Here, consider what goes wrong will.

12. **Include an underdog situation.** Everyone cheers for the underdog.

13. **Create Tension.** There must be a reason for the action or fight.

I like to use the following format when writing an action sequence or fight scene.

Initial Confrontation – Set up – Complication – Action – Response - Outcome

As a bonus to your action scene, consider adding combatants, changing weapons, or finding something in the environment, MacGyver style, for a change of pace or changing the terrain.

CHAPTER TWELVE

Showing vs. Telling

Since the beginning, authors have been taught to show rather than tell when writing their narratives. For example, Russian playwright Anton Chekhov said, "Don't tell me the moon is shining, show me the glint of the light on the broken glass." Chekhov attributed to the concept of showing rather than telling.

What exactly does that mean? When a writer tells a reader something, they use exposition, summaries, blunt descriptions, and rambling to convey the message, present the character, or activate a plot. This isn't ideal as it doesn't offer much for the reader as you are telling them by informing them instead of allowing them to deduce and experience the event by painting vivid scenes and reactions.

However, showing creates a dynamic manuscript and engages the reader into your story. It paints a picture for your reader in their mind's eye. In a nutshell, the big difference between showing and telling is that showing will use descriptions and actions to enhance the story. It creates ambiguity for the reader because they experience the story instead of being told by the author. The key to successful showing is to weave your story so that the reader is brought into the smell, sights, sounds, feelings, emotions without the author making it obvious; thus, keeping the reader interested and wanting to find out what happens next. Each detail brings life to the character and moves the plot forward.

Mastering the art of showing isn't that easy, but not that difficult either. To master this skill, here are eight tips.

1. Incorporate the character's five senses. No, you don't always have to use all five, e.g., sight, sound, touch, taste, and smell. However, you might overdo it if you do, so be selective and make each word impactful to bring the story alive.

2. As with all writing, use strong verbs and not weak ones. Strong verbs guide a reader into the senses.

3. Don't use adverbs. That's right, adverbs are useless and are considered a lazy way to write.

4. Write for specificity. This is to write what you mean for the reader to experience.

5. The key to successful showing is to focus on the actions and reactions of the characters.

6. Create a mental image for the reader.

7. Use lots of dialogue. The way for a reader to identify with a character is through their dialogue.

8. Avoid extemporaneous details that do not move the plot forward.

The Nuts and Bolts of Showing

The reasons for showing rather than telling include:

1. It allows readers to experience what the characters do and gets them close to the action.

2. It gives the readers specific details about a character.

3. It creates the tone and mood of the narrative.

4. Provides concrete imagery.

Here we go. It's time to learn how to write for showing rather than telling. Let's start with an emotion -- angry. Consider the sentence below.

> *Mary was very angry. She raised her voice and then lifted her fists.*

With the above sentences, it is telling rather than showing. It doesn't do much to the narrative because it is exposition. To show rather than tell, start with the word angry. How do you know Mary is angry? Because I told you. Wait. What happens if I show you that Mary is angry? Look at the revision below.

> *Mary's face turned crimson as she clenched her fists; her knuckles turned white. "I find this disgusting," she gagged, averting her eyes to catch her breath as she felt the blood pulse through her veins. "Just stop!" Mary pounded her fists against the table.*

In the example above, I refrained from using adverbs and never used the word angry. As a result, a reader learns Mary is angry because of her visceral reactions and actions. That is the key to effective showing over telling. Another example is when we describe one person's height to another. It isn't necessary to say that Bob is taller than Michael by a few inches. Instead, we put in a reaction and action for Bob and Michael. Look at this example.

> *Bob, about five inches taller than Michael, walked over and shook his hand.*

This sentence tells rather than shows. Now read the revision.

> *Bob strolled to Michael, gazing down at his blue eyes. It was a difficult reach to shake his hand.*

After reading the above sentence, you know several things. First, Bob is taller because he gazed down at his eyes and had difficulty shaking Michael's hand. Why? The height difference without me writing is that Bob is taller than Michael.

How to Show an Emotion

Complication arises when authors must explain or show the emotions of characters. It is too easy to write that a character is happy, sad, angry, hurt, in love, frustrated, scared, terrified, etc., but not so easy to show those feelings.

Here is what I mean.

> **Telling:** Janice was sad.
> **Showing:** Tears streaked Janice's flushed cheeks.

Telling: Blythe was happy with her new puppy.
Showing: An enormous grin graced Blythe's lips as she cuddled her adorable puppy.

Telling: Peter was angry at his opponent.
Showing: Peter's eyes narrowed as he slammed his fist on the podium.

Telling: The woman was crying at the funeral.
Showing: The woman's eyes welled as she slumped over the casket.

How to Rewrite a Telling Sentence

Specific phrases quickly identify a telling sentence. Consider:

- I heard
- I felt
- I smelled
- I touched
- I tasted

What is evident to you in the above? They identify the five senses. That's the key to identifying weakly written telling areas -- look for the five senses. Then, to improve your writing to showing, use the word search in your Word document for those, and then modify the sentence to show rather than tell.

Telling: I heard the baby cry from the next room.
Showing: The colic screams drifted down the hall.

Telling: I felt her hand gently touch mine.
Showing: Her scaly fingers rested on my balmy hand.

Telling: The smell of the cookies baking made me hungry.

Showing: Cinnamon filled the air tantalizing my tastebuds as my stomach growled.

Telling: I touched the scratch-off lottery ticket, revealing I won five dollars.

Showing: My heart raced as I scratched the slick, silver spot on the lottery ticket, revealing I won five dollars.

Telling: The lemon was bitter to the baby as he bit the rind.
Showing: The baby shivered as he bit the lemon rind.

Here are tips to effectively write showing sentences.

1. **Describe the senses.** Review your manuscript and identify the above sensory key phrases, identifying your telling sentences and then rewrite them to include vivid imagery. For example, if you heard a cry, what type was it? How loud? Who was crying? Why were they crying? Give us the details. If the character smells something, describe it.

2. Describe the character's visceral reactions. Include what is going on with the character on the inside. Think in terms of the heart rate, blood flowing through the body, temperature, etc.

3. Describe the character's body language. Don't limit yourself to facial expressions because that becomes dull. Include what the hands, feet, chest, does too. But not all at once.

4. Describe the character's actions. Did they stand, sit, jump, kick, leap, faint, etc.

5. Use strong verbs, always. Avoid using walk, run, chew, etc. Replace weak verbs with strong ones.

6. Describe the environment. Try to find something in the environment that is unique and interesting. If you can't, then don't bother. What makes the living room unique? Does it have peeling wallpaper; original artwork, self-portraits, framed newspaper articles, sporting equipment, trophies, toys, etc.,

Acceptable Uses of Telling

Occasionally telling rather than showing is acceptable, but rarely. For instance, authors tell in a short story when they need to limit their words and if they need to offer a quick summary. Useful telling exposition occurs when you want to describe an action that doesn't need an individual scene or if you want to introduce general information into something specific. But, again, use it sparingly.

TIP 5: I have several writing files I developed and refer to that help me include word lists. Start your file lists and refer to them often.

CHAPTER THIRTEEN

Overcoming Writer's Block

I think I can write. I think I can write. Nope, not today. Yikes! I have writer's block. Hold on for a minute. Did you know that writer's block isn't a medical condition that you can have a doctor prescribe medication to treat it? It isn't a disease at all. It is a mental block a writer imposes on themselves for various reasons. Consider the following:

- I am stressed, so I can't write.
- I seem to write the same old thing; I need something new.
- I have too much on my mind to write.
- I don't have time to write.
- Nobody will like what I'm writing, so why write?
- My mind is blank.

Whoa! Those are all excuses that you believe are true. They dictate what you think you will write today or tomorrow, or next week and fall into one of three categories.

- **Perfectionism** – When you think everything has to be perfect, you make excuses not to write. For instance, when you think, "Nobody will like what I'm writing, so why write?"
- **Fear of Failure** – We all experience fear, but when you let fear impede your accomplishments in writing, you get writer's block. So often, fear of failure is disguised as stress, in my layman's opinion. So be bold, brave, and write.
- **Lack of Time** – Okay, you might have me here. Our schedules are all tied up with jobs, family, and health issues. But, if writing is important, you will set a time to write, even if it is only five minutes.

How to Overcome Writer's Block

The first thing to do to get over writer's block is to acknowledge that it is all in your mind. Yep, it really is. You can write, or you wouldn't have started your novel or manuscript. That means you have to believe in yourself and forget about making excuses about not writing. I know that is easier said than done.

Let me help you out of this mental writer's block thing. No, I'm not a psychiatrist or a medical doctor, so I'm not giving you that kind of advice. Then again, since writer's block isn't a medical condition, a doctor couldn't prescribe something, anyway. Here is my advice on overcoming writer's block.

1. **Take a breather.** I mean, inhale slowly and exhale slowly about ten times. When you do this, think of a place that inspires you. I consider this my mental vacation. As writers, we can go anywhere we want using our imaginations. Use this to overcome writer's block. After your short mental vacation, write one sentence about where you went in your mind's eye. Then a second of what you saw. And then describe what you smelled, who you met, etc. Before you know it, you're writing again. Use this same method when stuck in your novel. Send your character on a mental vacation and tap into that.
2. **Exercise.** That means get up and move. Stretch, swim, ride a bike, or walk around the block. Remember that your brain is a muscle; when you stimulate other muscles in exercising, you're stimulating your brain too.
3. **Do something else creative.** I am a firm believer that creativity breeds creativity. When I experience writer's block, I will play the piano and compose music. I am also an artist, so I will also draw or paint. Usually, these

activities give me a break from writing, but as I compose or paint, I think of a scene in my next novel, and somehow ideas develop. You can listen to music and dance if you're not a musician. If you're not an artist, there are adult coloring books to color and be creative. That is how I ended up publishing six adult coloring books. After years, I realized I had enough drawings.

4. **Read**. When you read, you become inspired. So, simply escape into another book.

5. **Look around and find inspiration**. Your following sentence is waiting for you to write, and the inspiration is likely in front of you. For instance, I have a 1960s lava lamp on my desk that I find inspiration from. How? When I get stuck, I watch the lava part move up and down and start describing it in my mind. Then, I'm unstuck. Also, if I get stuck on naming a character, I'll look around the room. Once I saw my granddaughter's bright green glass. That inspired me to name a character after it. Mr. Glass became a name for one of the schoolteachers. So again, look around your environment for inspiration.

6. **Use the ABCs to write**. When stuck on what to write, use the alphabet to your advantage. This is a simple process to get you to write again. Let me show you how. This is much like *Scattergories.* First, you will choose a category, such as a person, place, or thing. For this example, I am going to choose things vegetables. So, I start with the letter 'A' and write about a vegetable that starts with that letter and try to use three other words with 'A.' Look at my first example.

   'A' - The **asparagus** is **absolutely awful**. Then move to the letter 'B.' **Broccoli** is **bitter** when **butter** isn't basted on it. All right, not the most brilliant, but I'm writing at least. 'C' - **Carrots** are always **cute** when they are **cut** small and are **crisp**. Oh, time to move on. I hope you get the idea. Usually, I make it to 'F' before going back to writing my manuscript. I think this works because it frees your mind and allows you to get silly without worrying that others are going to judge you.

7. **Be playful**. Sometimes as writers, we take ourselves too seriously. Have some fun and be a kid again. As crazy as it sounds, playing a board game, or *Solitaire*, or *Pictionary*. How? You are using your mind. I love to play with my grandchildren to overcome writer's block. We play, *Let's Write a Story*. Here are the rules. I have eight grandchildren, so it's easy for me to play. We sit in a circle, and one at a time, we answer the following questions.

    - Who is the story going to be about?
    - Where is this person going?
    - How are they going to get there?
    - What will they see on the way?
    - What will they do once they get there?
    - Who do they meet?
    - What do they do together?
    - What is their plan to meet again before they say goodbye?

Once we have answered those questions, I tell the story using their ideas. We have done it so many times; I now put them into writing and have published a book together called *The Creek Dweller in the Bayou*.

The cover is from the book we created together and all of the children pictured are the cartooned version of my grandkids. We had so much fun creating this book we are now working on a collection of their short stories and will publishing these soon under the banner of Absolute Author Publishing House's Children's Division.

CHAPTER FOURTEEN

Editing

Your first draft is never perfect. Remember that. To hone your draft requires editing, then editing, and re-editing. Editing is a skill that all writers must have, no matter what. There are five types of editing.

1. **Editorial Review/Assessments** – This type of editing offers broad feedback during the early development stage of writing. They help an author gain clarity and direction and provide insight into your writing strengths and weaknesses to hone your craft.

2. **Developmental Editing** – This type of editing involves the editor identifying plot holes and character development. This is a way for authors to get the "big picture" for their manuscripts. A developmental edit is also known as content or substantive editing.

3. **Copy Editing** – This type of editing focuses on spelling, grammar, and other technical issues such as sentence

structure. The editor will assess inconsistencies in spelling, style, typography, confusing sentences, etc.

4. **Fact-checking** – A fact-checker editor will review your material for accuracy to ensure that the information is correct in your manuscript.

5. **Proofreading** – This type of editing is usually the last editing to ensure that your manuscript is error-free before publication.

Listed below are the most common editing mistakes writers make.

1. Poorly punctuated,
2. Grammar mistakes,
3. Misspelling words,
4. Typos,
5. Word omissions,
6. Dialogue tags,

7. Usage of numbers or numerals,
8. POV/Tense,
9. Misusing the wrong word,
10. Structural mishaps, including sentence and paragraph structure,
11. Relying on software and author tools for editing,
12. Not editing, and
13. Not hiring a professional editor.

The errors mentioned above can and should be fixed. Every writer should have in their arsenal a strong background in grammar rules. However, never rely solely on software, thinking it will fix everything for you. They don't. Plug-ins, unfortunately, will not find all of your errors; however, they can assist you with your pacing, momentum, dialogue, word choice, redundancy, identifying passive voice, cliches, and filler words. I highly recommend that authors use editing software but choose wisely to accept the changes software suggests. The most used editing software includes:

- Autocrit
- Editminion
- Grammarly
- Hemingway Editor
- MasterWriter
- ProWritingAid
- SmartEdit
- WriteMonkey

I prefer ProWritingAid and Grammarly. I use a combination as each provides something different.

TIP 6: Never rely solely on editing software because they cannot find everything and cannot replace the human factor of a professional editor. For example, it will overlook their, there, and they're because all are spelled correctly. However, did you use them correctly?

Is Hiring a Professional Editor Worth it?

Often as writers, we type so fast that our fingers don't keep up with our brains. That's when it happens. You spell out a word and move on. Then, when you edit your work, your eyes move right on by, and you never see those pesky homonyms or those missing words that should have been in the sentence. I've done it, and authors do it. That is why you need to edit, edit, and edit your manuscript before publishing it. Here is the tricky part. Most authors don't have the finances or luxury to spend on a professional editor. I say you don't have the luxury of not hiring one. My reasons are simple and listed below.

- Your family and friends may have your best interest at heart, but they rarely understand the formatting and issues surrounding your manuscript. I have discovered that they aren't as ruthless as editors because they think you are the best thing since sliced bread and will overlook errors. Now, if your aunt or mother is an English professor, you stand a better chance. They will at least catch your grammatical errors and spelling. However, unless they have been in the publishing industry, they don't know what it takes to perfect a manuscript.

- You need an objective pair of eyes on your manuscript. Objectivity is the key when editing. If you self-edit, it is difficult to cut your own words. I've been there and done that. A professional editor won't hold back. They are not worried about hurting your feelings. Their concern is to edit, find those pesky mistakes, find the gaps in your plot, and make suggestions. Depending on the type of editor you hire, they may go as far as rewriting sentences or entire paragraphs. Your family and friends won't do that.
- Editors read differently from writers. As an author, we skip words and simply miss them when there should be a word. It is as if we speed read instead of reading to find errors. Editors are trained to find those pesky missing words in a sentence, grammatical errors, complex sentences, run-on sentences, and more.
- You save valuable time by hiring a professional editor. It took me two months to write *The Keystroke Killer: Transcendence*. It took me ten months to edit. The writing part was simple. Editing not so much. I don't edit my final draft, and I have a Ph.D. I am too close to my work to edit my manuscript. However, I learned when turning over my manuscript to a professional editor. I saved lots of hours. Those hours gave me the time to draft my next novel. That way, my time was spent wisely.

- A professional editor brings collaboration. Collaboration enhances your novel. Remember, two heads are better than one with editing. A great editor will make suggestions for improvement that you might have overlooked.
- When you work with a professional editor, you are mastering the craft of writing. You learn by reviewing their work, and then you don't make the same mistakes.
- Your reputation depends on it. The last thing any author needs is for your novel to be full of errors. Nothing makes a reader close your book faster than a poorly written, unedited manuscript. The damage will already be done as they are more than likely never to purchase any book written by you in the future.

I hear your pain with finances, but as a writer, you owe it to yourself and your readers to publish the best manuscript possible. I strongly recommend you start a saving account when writing your first novel. Don't purchase that extra cup of coffee. Instead, put that money aside and stash it away. You're going to need money to pay an editor and hire a graphic designer to make your book cover, a video production company for a trailer, and marketing materials. This all is a part of being an author.

Vetting Editors

Not all editors are created equal, and not all editors do all types of editing. Some specialize in copy and line editing, while others focus on developmental or proof editing. Therefore, it is essential to vet an editor. When vetting an editor, always ask for a free sample edit of a couple of paragraphs and make sure they track all edits. Also, remember that editing is a subjective process, and you do not have to accept all the recommended edits. It is your book and needs to reflect your voice. No matter how good the professional editor is, they can't turn a poorly written manuscript into a bestselling one. That is your job. Editors work within the confines of your words. When vetting an editor, follow these recommendations.

1. Make sure the editor is qualified. An English teacher isn't necessarily a great editor. Check the editor's experience and qualifications.

2. Investigate other books that the editor has edited. For example, you can go to Amazon and type in the editor's name, and books will come up, or ask them for a list.

3. Ask what genres the editor prefers and if they have experience in your genre.

4. Find out if they only rely on editing software; if so, run.

5. Determine if they outsource the edits.

TIP 7: When I first started vetting editors, I always sent them several manuscript pages and made certain I had specific errors for them to find, which included misused homonyms, misspelled words, lack of punctuation, wrong punctuation for dialogue, numbers that should be spelled out, etc. Further, I sent the same sample to each editor to compare their editing skills.

Ways to Make the Most from the Editing Process

The hardest thing for authors to forget is that their book is being edited. When you send your manuscript to an editor, forget about it until they return it to you. You don't want to add something and not have it edited. So, be patient. Instead, use your time to create your marketing plan or start outlining your next book.

Once you receive your edited manuscript, review all the edits, and learn from them. Also, remember that you don't have to accept the changes that an editor made; it is your book.

TIP 8: Always date your version of your manuscript as well as include the editor's first name in the file title. That way, you will always work from the latest manuscript and avoid confusion. For example, for this book, I had my two top editors, Kathy and Paul, with Absolute Author Publishing House edit it. I first used Kathy and had her track her changes, and then I reviewed those. Before sending it to Paul, I checked it, made necessary changes, accepted all tracked changes, and then sent the manuscript to him. I named each file differently.

Take_Control_Kathyedit.10.22.2021
Take_Control_Melreview.11.7.2021
Take_Control_Pauledit.12.2.2021
Tale_Control_Finaledit.1.7.2022

CHAPTER FIFTEEN

Dr. Mel's Editing Pet Peeves

That vs. Who

When editing, one of my pet peeves is the misuse of the words "that" and "who." When writing, the word "who" always refers to people, whereas the word "that" refers to animals, things, groups, buildings, etc. (nouns). These are the rules.

Consider the following:

> **Wrong:** Maggie is the one **that** scored the final basket, winning the game for our team.
>
> **Corrected:** Maggie is the one **who** scored the final basket, winning the game for our team.
>
> **Wrong:** April belongs to the New Orleans Writer's Association who supports her creativity.
>
> **Corrected:** April belongs to the New Orleans Writer's Association **that** supports her creativity.

That vs. Which

Using "that" over "which" has long caused nightmares for writers. Which one do you use? Are they interchangeable? Traditionally, the use of "that" occurs with restrictive clauses and "which" with nonrestrictive ones. What is the difference between a restrictive and nonrestrictive clause?

A restrictive clause narrows the subject to a single one. For example, look at the following restrictive clause.

> *The picture that hangs in the foyer is my mother.*

Here, we are referencing one picture: thus, the use of that. It singles it out. If over one painting hung in the foyer, then this would be a nonrestrictive use as it references over one painting.

> *The pictures which hang in the foyer are my parents.*

To further help you, most writers use "that" for inanimate objects or groups and "which" for relative pronouns for humans.

TIP 9: Go through your manuscript and search for the word "that," "who," and "which" and make sure you have used them correctly.

Homonyms, Homophones, and Homographs

No matter how good of a writer you are, using the wrong homonym occurs. Unfortunately, spellcheck programs don't pick these up either, so it takes a thorough review of your manuscript. A homonym is two or more words that sound the same sound or spelling but have different meanings, such as principal and principle. Homophones are spelled differently, such as knew and new, their, there, and they're, bare and bear, etc., but sound the same. Homographs are words that sound the same but differ in origin or meaning, such as bear and bare. It is essential that you know the meaning of each word and how to use it correctly.

Listed below are the most confused homonyms, homophones, and homographs.

Accept – Except
Ad – Add
Advice – Advise
Aid – Aide
Ail – Ale
Air – Ere
Aisle – I'll – Isle
Allusion – Illusion
Alter – Altar
Bale – Bail
Band – Banned
Beat – Beet
Blue – Blew
Buy – By – Bye
Capital – Capitol
Cell – Sell
Cent – Scent – Sent
Cereal – Serial
Chews – Choose
Chile – Chili – Chilly
Chord – Cord
Cite – Site – Sight
Close – Clothes
Coarse – Course
Complement – Compliment
Council – Counsel
Creak – Creek
Crews – Cruise
Days – Daze
Dear – Deer
Desert – Dessert
Dew – Do – Due

Die – Dye
Discreet – Discrete
Doe – Dough
Dual – Duel
Elicit – Illicit
Eminent – Imminent
Facts – Fax
Fair – Fare
Fairy – Ferry
Faze – Phase
Fir – Fur
Flea – Flee
Flour – Flower
For – Four – Fore
Forward – Foreword
Gorilla – Guerilla
Gray- Grey
Grease – Greece
Groan – Grown
Hall – Haul
Hay – Hey
Heal – Heel
Hear – Here
Hoarse – Horse
Hole – Whole
Holey – Holy – Wholly
Knead – Need
Knew – New
Knot – Not
Know – No
Lead – Led
Lesson – Lessen
Mail – Male
Marry – Merry
Meat – Meet
None – Nun
Oar – Or – Ore
One – Won
Overdo – Overdue
Pail – Pale
Pain – Pane
Peace – Piece
Peak – Peek - Pique
Patience – Patients
Pear – Pair
Plain – Plane
Pole – Poll
Poor – Pour
Pray – Prey
Principal – Principle
Rain – Rein
Rap – Wrap
Read – Red
Real – Reel
Road – Rode
Role – Roll
Scene – Seen
Sea – See
Seam – Seem
Sew – So – Sow
Soar – Sore
Sole – Soul
Son – Sun
Some – Sum
Stair – Stare
Steal – Steal
Suite – Sweet
Tail – Tale
Their – There – They're
Threw – Through

To – Too – Two
Toe- Tow
Vary – Very
Wail – Whale
Waist – Waste
Wait – Weight
War – Wore
Warn – Worn
Way – Weigh
We – Wee
Weak – Week
Wear – Where
Weather – Whether
Which – Witch
Wood – Would
Your – You're

TIP 10: When in doubt of which form of a word to use, always look up the definition. Consider the definitions and how they are used.

Modifiers

Modifiers drive me crazy. A modifier is a phrase or clause placed in a sentence, which appears to modify or refer to an unintended word. When a modifier is misused, it confuses or skews the sentence's meaning. A modifier adds information or changes the nature of the information in the sentence without altering the grammatical structure. Usually, misplaced modifiers are adjectives, adverbs, phrases, or clauses. A pre-modifier is positioned before the word and are usually adjectives coming before a noun. Adverbs are also frequently positioned before the verb. A post-modifier is placed after the subject or object of the sentence. Here are the different modifiers to be weary of using.

Dangling Modifier

A dangling modifier is one where the word or phrase is not associated with the subject rather than the object of the sentence and is the most common error writers make.

Here is a perfect example.

The woman was pulled over by the state trooper in the red car.

Wait, who is in the red car? The state trooper or the woman? In this example, the woman is; however, the sentence is confusing because the words "in the red car" are misplaced and do not modify the woman's car. This is called post-modifier.

The state trooper pulled over the woman in the red car.

Limiting Modifier

When a writer imposes limits on a pronoun, subject, or noun, it is called a limiting modifier. Limiting modifiers are easily recognized because they usually contain the words simply, hardly, at first, or just. When a limiting modifier is used, the sentence's meaning can change, again creating confusion. Look at this example.

Just Kathy eats popcorn as a snack.

What is the meaning of this sentence? Does it mean that the only person in the world who eats popcorn as a snack is Kathy? Not at all. Now consider this revision.

Kathy eats only popcorn as a snack.

Much clearer. We know that the only snack Kathy eats is popcorn.

TIP 11: To avoid misplaced, dangling, or limiting modifiers in your writing, place the modifier in the appropriate place to convey the meaning you intend in the sentence. In essence, closest to the verb or name you desire to modify.

Words to Capitalize in Titles, Subtitles, Headings, and Subheadings

When to Capitalize

There are many confusing rules on what words to capitalize in a title or heading. One mistake authors make when writing manuscripts is to follow either APA or Chicago Style rules. This isn't the case for fiction and for the most part, nonfiction such as memoirs. Always remember that your manuscript isn't an academic paper or an English essay unless you are publishing it as such. That means that everything you thought you knew goes out the window. I always adhere to the rules submitted by the *New York Times* because they set the new-age standard for capitalization in the publishing world.

Always capitalize the following:

- The first and last word in the title, regardless of the part of speech
- Proper nouns, nouns, pronouns, verbs, and adverbs
- Subordinate conjunctions (as, because, although)

List of Words not Capitalized

Do not capitalize the following:

- Articles (a, an, the)
- Short words (fewer than four letters)
- Prepositions (at, by, to, etc.)
- Coordinating Conjunctions (and, but, for)

The Number Dilemma

Nothing drives me crazier when I edit or read a book than to find numbers or numerals that should have been spelled. Again, the AP and Chicago Style goes out the window. You were taught that numerals below nine are spelled in English class, and those above aren't. Not so in fiction writing.

Numbers vs. Numerals

Numerals are usually phone numbers, seat numbers, odd dollar amounts, dates, etc. In these instances, it is best not to spell them out. On the other hand, numbers sometimes get spelled, and some don't. There are rules to follow; however, there are exceptions to the rules as fast as there are rules. Here are the rules to follow.

1. Numbers one to one hundred – write them out unless they appear at the beginning of a sentence or are included in a date.

   Wrong: 5 cats hissed at the puppy.
   Correct: Five cats hissed at the puppy.

   Wrong: When I was 50, I realized that I had lived for 5 decades.
   Correct: When I was fifty, I realized that I had lived for five decades.

2. Use numerals for 101 and above.

   Wrong: My book, *A.D.A.M.* was published in 24 languages and was one of 800 to make the bestsellers list in those countries.
   Correct: My book, *A.D.A.M.* was published in twenty-four languages and was one of 800 to make the bestsellers list in those countries.

3. Round numbers should always be spelled out.

   Wrong: Stephen Hawking wrote three hundred books and over 100,000 articles.
   Correct: Stephen Hawking wrote three hundred books and over one hundred thousand articles.

4. Numbers in dialogue are always spelled no matter what.

   Wrong: "I found out that I have 120 pairs of shoes."
   Correct: "I found out that I have one hundred and twenty pairs of shoes."

5. When writing ordinal numbers, e.g., 2nd, 5th, etc., the rule one above applies.

   Wrong: I was born on January 1st, 1958.
   Correct: I was born on January 1, 1958.

6. When writing decades, e.g., 1920s, an apostrophe is not needed.

   Wrong: The 1920's witnessed vast changes to woman's clothing designs.
   Correct: The 1920s witnessed vast changes to woman's clothing designs.

7. Roman numerals may be used in personal names but should be avoided in dialogue.

   Wrong: John Paul the Second is a distinguished man.
   Correct: John Paul II is a distinguished man.

8. When writing symbols such as '$' or '%,' it is acceptable to do so except if they occur in dialogue and must be spelled out, e.g., dollar and percent.

   Wrong: "I earned an 80% commission on the sale of my book."
   Correct: "I earned an eighty percent commission on the sale of my book."

9. When writing dates, don't use the ordinal number.

   Wrong: Elvis Presley was born on January 8th, 1935.
   Correct: Elvis Presley was born on January 8, 1935.

10. To correctly write the time, use the following format: 7:30 a.m. It is unnecessary to add another period to the end of that sentence. Also, if referring to a clock, you must spell out that number. For instance, it was seven o'clock when the doorbell rang.

    Wrong: I plan on getting up at 6:00 AM.
    Correct: I plan on getting up at 6:00 a.m.
    Correct: I plan on getting up at six in the morning.

11. To correctly write height, never use 5'4." Instead, spell those out as five foot four inches.

    Wrong: The petite model was 5'4" and very pretty.
    Correct: The petite model was five foot four inches and very pretty.

12. When referring to weapons, always include the numbers and spell them like the manufacturer.

    Wrong: The soldier maneuvered the Nr.Five Armata tank through the minefield.
    Correct: The soldier maneuvered the Nr.5 Armata tank through the minefield.

CHAPTER SIXTEEN

Formats

Now that your manuscript is ready, what is the next step? Do you publish the book as an eBook, paperback, hardback, and audio? Or, do you choose only one format? Each format requires a distinct ISBN.

Although you can publish an eBook without an ISBN, I recommend you obtain one, anyway, to solidify your work. In an earlier chapter, I discussed formatting in Word for the paperback and hardback. But, is that the only software you need? Unfortunately, no. You also need to convert your manuscript into other formats, especially the eBook. Listed below are the best software to use to convert your eBook.

- **Apple Pages** - Exports EPUB files
- **Blurb** - Creates print + digital full-color books
- **Book Creator** - iPad app to generate illustrated books
- **Calibre** - Free software useful for file conversion to/from EPUB. It can be but difficult to use with a large learning curve.
- **Draft2Digital** – Software that you can upload your Word doc for EPUB conversion.
- **KDP Kids' Book Creator** – Used for creating children's picture books. Does require technical savvy.
- **Kindle Create** - A program developed by Amazon to convert a Word document into an eBook. It is user-friendly, and the learning curve is small.
- **PressBooks** - a WordPress-based platform for creating both EPUB and print files.
- **Scrivener** - Software is not free, but it can export EPUB files. There is a learning curve to use this as it isn't always user-friendly.
- **Sigil** - Software for producing EPUB files with a large learning curve.
- **Reedsy** - A free online editor to export EPUB files. A strong learning curve.
- **Vellum** - Software for Mac users only to produce EPUB files. It is user-friendly.

There are six major distributors for your eBook.

- **Amazon** – Probably sells 93% of all eBooks and is the distribution channel I prefer.
- **Apple Books** – Widely considered the No. 2 eBook retailer in the U.S.
- **Barnes & Noble Nook Press** – A viable option, although sales have plummeted on that platform because of the competition of Amazon.
- **Kobo** – Has an international presence.
- **Smashwords** – One of the largest eBook distributors of self-published titles. They do charge you part of your royalty.
- **Draft2Digital** – A company that is gaining ground. They take a part of your royalty.

If you don't want to create the eBook and desire help, my company offers that. You can find a complete list of my services in the Appendix. You can also go to Fiverr and find a freelancer.

Optimizing Your Product Description

Without a strong product description, readers are likely to bypass purchasing your book. Think about it. The description and the cover are the first things a reader reviews. If they are turned off by a poorly written description filled with grammatical and typing errors, they move on. One of the hardest parts of publishing and distribution is writing your description. Don't rush writing your description and hone it until it is perfect. You have two hundred words to make an impact, so choose your words wisely. It is ill-advised to write something longer.

Your description should summarize your book, which includes hooks, the story's plot points. I always suggest that you write several versions of your description and allow your friends, family, and colleagues to provide feedback. Often, they will see something you didn't allow, and you can adjust. The key is to keep it short and succinct. Tips for writing a powerful description.

1. Search categories and find the best viable one for your book.

2. Use your keywords in your description and any bullet points.

3. Look for themes on Amazon. Determine the hot themes and adjust your description.

4. Make sure your title stands out by creating a dynamic headline.

Categories and Keywords

Assigning the correct categories and using impactful keywords is essential and should never be overlooked. Marketing and social media can only do so much to drive sales. Categories help readers locate your book according to the topic, whereas keywords will aid them in searching for your book. Consider both a browsing pathway, a roadmap for readers. The categories are based on BISAC categories, an industry standard for subject headings for most distribution companies. I suggest an author go to Amazon and research books in the genre and look at the categories assigned. Discover those that are bestselling, and then be selective when assigning yours. Ideally, choose a category with limited books to limit your competition.

Keywords are essentially your guidepost and are key phrases that will target your readers. Be selective. Again, search for other books and their keywords.

CHAPTER SEVENTEEN

Audiobooks

Audible books or audiobooks are popular in the market. It is almost a must for an author to remain competitive in the market. So, move over eBooks and paperbacks; the audiobook is taking over.

Research indicates that audiobooks are the fastest-growing market for authors, so it's time to get on board. As frustrating and challenging as it may sound, it is easier than you think. According to *The Wall Street Journal*, audiobooks are a $2.5 billion industry. Why? They are convenient, and readers who commute listen to their books, and not read them. It's easy on the eyes in a world where the computer screen and cell phones are a massive part of our culture. If you want to expand your reader base, one of the quickest ways is to turn your novel into an audiobook.

Why are Audiobooks Growing?

There are a variety of reasons for audiobook growth. Consider these:

1. Readers are constantly on the go using various modes of transportation:
    - Walking
    - Jogging
    - Running
    - Cars
    - Planes
    - Trains
    - Spaceflights (Okay, only a handful)
2. Although audiobooks have been around for some time, readers want them more today than ever. Unfortunately, that means you need to convert your novel to meet the supply and demand.
3. It may be difficult to comprehend, but some people love books who cannot read. Audiobooks make it easy for a

blind person to get involved or a person who is not in the position to read for themselves. I remember when I was so sick in the hospital, I couldn't hold my head up, couldn't watch television because of my blurred vision, but I could listen to a powerful story in audiobook form. Others may not know how to read.

Why Convert Your E-Book into an Audiobook?

There is less competition for audiobooks than there are for paperbacks and eBooks, which means the potential for your earning power increases, and audiobooks never sell out. Also, the process is probably more straightforward than you imagine, with a variety of services at your disposal.

The Ways and Means to Convert Your Novel Into an Audiobook

There are a couple of ways:

- Have it produced; hire a voiceover narrator.
- Produce it yourself, hire the voiceover narrator and go to a recording studio.
- Produce it yourself, purchase the equipment, and narrate it yourself.
- Or a combination of the above.

That leaves you with the big question. Do you do it yourself or hire it done?

There are pros and cons to both. Of course, if you hire a producer, it will be professional, but it could be costly for the narrator and to rent the recording studio. The fees range depending on your area and could cost $1,000 or more. Ouch! What indie author can afford that?

The Basic Equipment

If you choose to produce it, you will have to purchase the equipment for quality control and be responsible for editing the final product. Wow! Before you get off this gravy train, it's not as expensive as you might think. Let me explain.

To produce your audiobook, you will need quality equipment. You probably already have a computer which is the largest expense. Here are the items you will need:

- A desktop computer, the newer, the better
- A quality XLR microphone
- A pop filter to cover the microphone
- A stand, preferably one that attaches to your desk
- A USB2 multi-mixer that connects my XLR mic to the USB port on your computer
- A quiet place to record with carpet to prevent noise bouncing from the floor
- Audacity (A free software program to record and edit your files. Click on the link to download it.)

Now you might think that sounds like a lot of money. Not really; one of my authors bought her entire equipment on Amazon -- a complete package for less than $100. She produced it herself, held narration auditions to find the perfect voice, although she could have read it herself and saved that money. Your goal is to research the equipment and find what you need.

Here is a package I found on Amazon. No, I don't get any money for promoting these packages; they are just examples.

Aokeo AK-70 Professional Studio Live Stream Broadcasting Recording Condenser Microphone With AK-35 Suspension Scissor Arm Stand, Shock Mount, Pop Filter, USB Sound Card, and Mounting Clamp. This complete system was under $80 and can be shipped to your home in less than three days.

Here is another brand, the Tonor Condenser Microphone set recording mic with a suspension book scissor arm stand with a built-in XLR cable and pop filter shock mount holder and a 48V phantom power supply with an adapter kit.

You will also need a pop filter shown below, ranging from $8 to $25.

There are dozens of more examples of equipment. Just do your due diligence to determine what will best fit your needs.

ACX

If you're not capable of narrating the book or simply don't want to, then ACX.com is the way to go. ACX is associated with Amazon and is the platform I use. I discovered many gifted narrators there, and I am incredibly pleased with the results. The advantage of using ACX to hire your narrator is that you maintain control, can approve of each chapter as you go, and you can either pay upfront for the cost of the production, share in royalties, or do a combination of both. Once completed, ACX uploads and connects your audiobook to your paperback, hardback, and eBook on Amazon. The process isn't difficult.

TIP 12: My audiobooks sell a hundred to one over my paperbacks and eBooks. It is well worth the time, effort, and investment.

CHAPTER EIGHTEEN

Publishing and Distribution

Aspiring authors are often confused about the distinction between publishing and distribution. They are two different things. A distributor is not a publisher, and a publisher is not a distributor. What's the difference? A publisher helps prepare the manuscript and prepare it for printing a distribution. They assign the ISBN, which allows the book to be sold. A distribution company prints the book and ships it. My mother always said, "All things in divine order," and this saying holds for publishing books as well. An overview of the publication and distribution process looks like this.

1. Create manuscript,
2. Format manuscript,
3. Edit, edit, and edit manuscript,
4. Revise manuscript,
5. Send the manuscript to Beta Readers,
6. Finalize manuscript,
7. Assign ISBN,
8. Design cover,

9. Copyright manuscript,
10. Upload for sale or presale,
11. Distribution begins, and
12. Market, market, market.

You have gone through drafting your manuscript, editing it, and re-editing it, and it is now time to publish your book. Here is the conundrum -- do you self-publish, traditionally publish, or use a hybrid? Each has pros and cons, and as the author, you need to do your research and decide which is the best route for you. Is there a right or wrong choice? That depends. You must be comfortable with your decision, as it affects the distribution channel. Prior research and publishing through the proper channels can ultimately save you headaches, heartaches, and trouble in the future. Seasoned writers are aware of the headaches, whereas aspiring authors are not. Let's discuss the alternatives available for publishing.

Self-publishing

What is self-publishing? Self-publishing is when an author prints and distributes their book through a platform, bypassing traditional publishing channels. This means they are responsible for every step, including editing, cover design, uploading, distribution, and marketing. I need to be clear on something. I do not believe in self-publishing, and I witness many authors who make serious mistakes when they decide to self-publish. Yes, you maintain complete control of everything; however, you also take many risks. Here are the downfalls of self-publishing.

1. **Aspiring authors publish too quickly.** Often, authors get antsy and what to publish their book right now. The problem is that the manuscript might not be ready. Before you hit the publish button, ask, "Is my book ready for the world to see?" When in

doubt, don't. You risk getting negative reviews. If you haven't had your manuscript professionally edited or formatted to industry standards, it will show, and your book will not sell. I admit completing the final editing is often a nightmare and isn't enjoyable for most authors. Did you know that most *New York Bestselling* authors say they edit their book at least fifty times before sending it to a professional editor? Remember, it is better to have patience and hire an editor than hit that publish button. You only get one chance at becoming the #1 New Release.

2. **Lack of credibility.** Self-published books don't have the best reputation, nor do self-published authors. I hate to say it, but readers often bypass self-published books because, in their minds, they lack credibility. They want to read something by an established author or one who warranted a publisher.

3. **Lack of fan base.** Self-published authors rarely have the fan base to get their book off the ground. It isn't easy establishing a fan base. It took me over twenty years to have a nine million-plus following on my blog, and that is with me authoring over ninety books.

4. **Solidified copyright.** When you self-publish, the book establishes copyright that is only associated with that book, which essentially means that another publishing company can't publish it. Once you go that route, there is no turning back.

5. **Ineligible for a bestseller.** Self-published authors aren't eligible for the *New York Time's Bestselling List* or *USA Today*. If that means nothing to you, then don't worry.

6. **It can be more expensive.** Aspiring authors make many mistakes and have to clean them up before moving forward. There is a strong learning curve for aspiring authors. Going with

a publisher can help you navigate the process for a successful outcome. When publishing, specific steps must be adhered to, or you risk failure and excess expenses.

7. **Distribution mistakes**. There is a considerable distinction between publishing and distribution. Aspiring authors get the notion that they will make more money by self-publishing. Often they hire a printing company to make hundreds of copies. Then, they try to sell them solely on their website and become the shipper and handler. Wait! This is very costly, and often authors end up with hundreds of unwanted books sitting in their offices or garages. Amazon sells over 93% of all books. The chances of you competing with Amazon are slim to none. They can print and distribute at a fraction of the cost through print on demand.

8. **Not sold in bookstores.** A bookstore will not carry a self-published book.

There are advantages to self-publishing, but not many.

1. **You maintain complete control.** There is something to be said about maintaining control of your work. However, is it worth it? Maintaining complete authority risks having an inferior book and potentially spending thousands of dollars wastefully. Instead of writing your next book, you must concentrate on selling the first one.

2. **Changes are easy.** When you are in control, any changes can easily be accomplished without going through the red tape of a traditional publisher.

3. **Profit margin.** Yes, when you self-publish, you keep nearly all of your profits by cutting the middleman. What you sell is yours. However, if no one knows who you are and can't find your book

because it is only on a website, your book will probably not sell. Ask yourself, "Would you rather earn less and sell more, or sell less and make nothing?"

4. **You're published.** When you self-publish, you don't have to worry about rejections from publishers, and you can publish your book as soon as you desire.

If you decide to self-publish, it's critical to research self-publishing platforms. Unfortunately, they are not all equal, and each has its requirements for submission. Therefore, it is essential to research each and determine if they fit your budget and needs before deciding on a platform. Services vary, as do the requirements for submission. Please know that the best services charge upfront and usually pass on the author's net sales. They make their money by offering editing, formatting, cover design, and marketing services. Be wary of those companies who use high-pressure sales tactics. Always read the fine print and do thorough research on each platform. Again, I don't believe in self-publishing as there are better alternatives.

Traditional Publishing

Traditional publishing can be troublesome, and there is no guarantee that your book will be distributed. When traditionally published, a gatekeeper guides you every step and often might change your manuscript. The drawback is that a traditional publisher doesn't provide a large royalty scale often, where an author earns less than fifteen percent. Ouch! However, there are many advantages.

1. **You gain instant credibility**. Readers love a book that someone else cares about publishing. The mindset is that it must be good since a publisher added it to their company. Therefore, it must be good, right?

2. **No upfront costs**. A traditional publisher pays for everything once you sign a binding contract, making it an affordable alternative.

3. **Hassle-free.** The publisher handles everything from editing, formatting, cover design, uploading, and marketing, freeing the author.

4. **Placement in bookstores.** Most traditional publishers have a distribution channel, especially in a brick-and-mortar store.

With everything, there are also cons to using a traditional publisher.

1. **You lose control.** The publisher will have the final say on the interior and manuscript. You may not like what they do to your work.

2. **Time is not your friend.** It takes time to find a traditional publisher that takes aspiring authors. Once signed, it can take up to a year to see your book for sale.

3. **Lower royalty.** Because of the upfront costs of publishing, a traditional publisher charges more in royalties.

4. **Lawyer needed.** The contracts with a traditional publisher are lengthy and filled with red tape. Therefore, it is advised that you present the contract to your entertainment attorney before signing it.

Hybrid Publishing

Hybrid publishing has taken off like a rocket to Mars and is a relatively new business model. It is one of the most misunderstood types of publishing for aspiring authors. Not to be confused with a hybrid author who uses self-publication and traditional publishing. Hybrid publishing is another form of self-publishing, but the author purchases services and the ISBN from the company. My company is a hybrid publishing company that allows authors to maintain control of their manuscripts while having the credibility of a publishing company behind them. I don't accept every manuscript, and an author isn't required to purchase any of our company's services. Here are the benefits of using a hybrid publishing company.

1. **Imprint.** You acquire an ISBN accepted worldwide with a publishing company imprint and logo.

2. **Services.** As the author, you choose how much and which service you need to distribute your book.

3. **Royalties.** Authors receive higher royalties. In my company, we do not take any royalties at all.

4. **Expertise.** Hybrid publishers offer expertise and experience for an aspiring author.

5. **Track record.** A hybrid company has a track record of publications.

6. **Success.** Success breeds success. Many hybrid publishers have bestselling authors, which is excellent news for an aspiring author. Readers often look for other books published by the same publishing company.

Why not Accept a Free ISBN

An ISBN is an acronym for International Standard Book Number -- a commercial identifier. It is a 10-13-digit number placed on the back cover of your book, identifying it to book dealers, wholesalers, warehouses, and retailers. This is how distributors identify books for sale. Every paperback and hardback must have one. They are assigned to text-based manuscripts or monographics other than journals, newspapers, or other types of serials. Once assigned, it can only be used for that book. Consider the ISBN like the book's passport. It identifies the book. Several companies offer free ISBNs if you decide to distribute with them. However, stay clear. Several complications surface. First, a free ISBN will not be assigned the EIN-5 barcode, which is the price tag for the book. This code must be assigned to your book to be sold in a bookstore. Second, if you accept a free ISBN, they will own your distribution rights and not you. Read their fine print. Also, you cannot sell your book in a bookstore. Finally, you cannot list your book on multiple channels if you accept a free ISBN.

Each ISBN consists of five elements.

1. **Prefix** – The prefix is usually three numbers at the beginning. Currently, those numbers start with either 978 or 979.

2. **Registration group** – The second set of numbers in the ISBN identifies the country or geographical region of the assigned imprint.

3. **Registrant** – The third set of numbers identifies the publisher or imprint and is usually seven digits.

4. **Publication** – This set of numbers identifies the edition or the format of the specific title.

5. **Check digit** – This is the last number in the series and mathematically validates the rest.

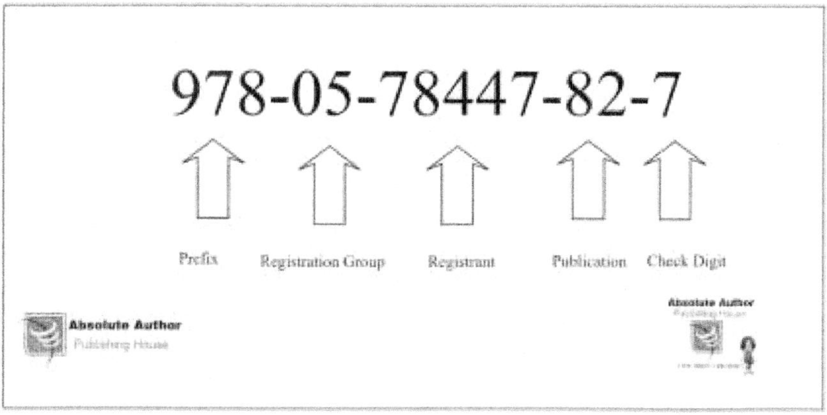

In America, ISBNs are only sold from Bowker Identifier Services. You can purchase them singularly at $125 or in bulk. Face it, this is a publishing cost, and there is no way around it. Again, once assigned to a title, it cannot be transferred.

In other countries, ISBNs are also available. For example, Neilson assigns them in the UK, and there is a cost associated. However, in Canada and India, the government issues them for free.

Bar Codes

The physical book's bar code is placed on the back cover of a paperback and hardback. Is it necessary to add it to the back cover during the cover design process? No, and here is why. I never put the bar code on the back cover and let the distributor add it. That way, I can use the cover for the hardback and paperback. Otherwise, it requires two covers. Then, if I decide to change my pricing, if the bar code is on the back cover, I will have to change the cover again. Therefore, it is easier to let the distribution company place them. However, if you insist on placing it on your back cover, free bar code generators are available, or you can get one from your publisher, who assigned the ISBN.

978-05-78447-82-7

Please know that by assigning an ISBN does not copyright your book. That is completed separately through the U.S. Library of Congress. Some countries require the ISBN to be a legal requirement, so contact your national ISBN agency for any clarification or legalities.

Establishing Price Point

Greedy author's books don't sell. Why? New authors overprice their books, knocking themselves out of the competition. As a new author, your words are not gold. You must keep in mind the concept of supply and demand. Again, your book competes with sixty million-plus books, and the pricing must be competitive. When I price my books, I strive to earn anywhere between $2.15 to $3.00 in royalty per book. That's it. No more, no less. Think in terms, would you instead sell more books and earn more, or fewer books and receive a higher royalty?

Distributing Through Multiple Channels

A huge mistake that aspiring authors make is in the beginning distributing their books on multiple platforms. The myth is that the more platforms your book is available, the more sales your book generates, leading to either a #1 New Release or a bestseller. Not so true. Don't fall into the trap of what you think all authors do. They aren't always on the correct path. Yes, seasoned authors distribute on multiple channels; however, for first-time authors, you will harm yourself. The fact is, when you distribute on multiple channels, e.g., Amazon, Kobo, Ingramspark, etc., you compete against yourself. Therefore, your sales will not accumulate into one. I only distribute on Amazon except for my hardbacks, where I go with Barnes & Noble Press because I like the quality of the hardback they print.

Don't get me wrong. There are advantages to distributing on multi-channels but at a later date.

1. **Customer perception.** Most customers perceive your book as successful when they see it available on multiple retailers' sites.

2. **Customer base.** The chances of increasing your customer base are greater as some readers only purchase their book from their preferred site or read in their subscription, such as Kindle.

Submitting to Absolute Author Publishing House

Are you looking for a publisher? If so, I would love for you to consider my company. If you followed my advice in this book, we would accept your publication. It is a win-win for you.

Here is the lowdown about Absolute Author Publishing House (AAPH). We believe the author should have absolute control over their book from the beginning to the end. It is your book, and it needs to remain that way. Dr. Carol Michaels and I founded the company based on this principle. Why? I have nightmare stories about my publishing journey with a traditional publisher, self-publishing, and hybrid author. I signed with a traditional publishing company when I published my first book. This was back in the late 1980s when the internet wasn't invented, nor was Amazon. The only option I had was to publish traditionally. To this day, I am still contracted with them and only earn 20% in royalties. Because I am a bestseller, they will not release my contract, and I can't sell those books on my website. That is why you don't see all ninety books on it.

My future changed in the 90s when Createspace came online with Amazon. I thought I had freedom. Wrong! I accepted a free ISBN and soon discovered that my books couldn't be sold in bookstores or placed in a library. That was a massive setback as most of my early books were educational for children. I had to do something but wasn't sure of my path. That's when Carol encouraged me to start a publishing company. We vowed not to do what traditional publishers did and take an author's royalties. Instead, we began one of the first hybrid publishing companies.

In the early days, we were confused with a vanity press. We're different in that you do not have to use our editing, graphic, or marketing services to publish with us, and we don't have a massive price tag for our services. If you have a quality manuscript, we are open to publishing as we have many divisions, such as a children's division. You might wonder how we make our money? Frankly, by offering services, but that isn't the criteria. Instead, we sell you the ISBN with our imprint, and you can use our logo to show that you are an Absolute Author. It is a win for you, and you have the best of both worlds.

TIP 13: Never rush to publication. If you do, you are more likely to make costly mistakes. Take your time. I always put my book to the side for about six weeks once I have finished with the last editing so that I can have a fresh perspective when I do the last review of it before publishing.

How to Submit to AAPH

If you are interested in submitting to AAPH, contact us at carol.absoluteauthor@gmail.com. Please write to us first and include your query letter and the first chapter to assess your manuscript.

You may also visit our website.

Absolute Author
Publishing House

https://absoluteauthorpuplishinghouse.com/

CHAPTER NINETEEN

Designing Your Cover

How exciting. You have finished your manuscript, and the next step is to have your cover designed. There are plenty of ways to accomplish this task. Keep in mind that a book cover must be eye-catching to captivate the reader's attention.

1. Use a software program to design your cover.
2. Hire a professional freelancer or cover designer.
3. Have a friend do it.
4. Hire a professional cover design company.

A book cover consists of three mandatory elements.

1. **The front cover** – to display the title, subtitle, and author.
2. **The back cover** – to present the book's description and information about the author.
3. **The spine** – to highlight the book title and author's name when on a shelf.

Mistakes Author Make With Book Covers

Book covers, when done correctly, can be your saving grace. One that is cumbersome or cluttered will be a distraction. There is a fine line. Here are the most common mistakes authors make when designing their covers.

1. They do not capitalize the correct words.
2. They put the title too close to the top or the edge, not leaving room for printing or binding.
3. They put the author's name too close to the bottom, again not leaving room for printing or binding.
4. They use sublime colors. A cover must pop in the presentation and stand out.
5. They use blurred graphics. Please invest in images and graphics in high resolution.
6. They don't consider their target audience or genre.
7. They choose an unattractive or unreadable font.

Cover Creator Software

If you are skilled in graphics, consider creating your cover. Below are six of the top software for doing such.

1. Canva.com
2. Picmonkey
3. Adobe InDesign
4. Book Brush

5. Blurb BookWright
6. Visme
7. Gimp

My Cover Designs

I have had plenty of experience designing book covers; however, that doesn't mean I design my own. I don't. I realize my limitations and skill set and prefer a professional to design my covers. Guess what? It doesn't cost me an arm and a leg. I found my cover designer on Fiverr. She is fantastic and is very reasonable, charging me $15 per cover. She has created at least thirty of my covers and hundreds for my clients at AAPH. Take advantage of this site. There are plenty of cover designers available.

TIP 14: A word of caution, do not have your cover designed before your book is completely finished and formatted because the cover must match the specification size of your book. If you create your cover too soon, it will not fit and must be redone, costing you more money. I always have at least two covers made so I can have options. Also, please know that each book format has different requirements for your cover and must be sized accordingly.

CHAPTER TWENTY

Dealing with Rejection

Most aspiring authors strive to obtain a literary agent or manager. But is it necessary, and is it worth it? The answer to these questions opens up a sore spot for many authors. Over the years, I have had many agents and managers. Of course, some were better than others. But, honestly, I make more money with my books, not involving a manager or agent, as I have taken control of my outcome. So, don't get discouraged if you can't obtain a literary agent.

How to Find a Literary Agent

Literary agents serve as a liaison between an author and publisher. Wait, if you self-publish or use a hybrid approach, you leave out the middleman and don't need one, and, frankly, they are challenging to find. Most literary agents don't accept unsolicited work or new authors. However, if you still desire to obtain one, you must start the query process to find representation or secure a publishing company. Agents charge for their services by taking a percentage of your royalties and earning a commission. Yikes! That's why I don't have one. However, if you choose to go this route, you must create a powerful cover letter and synopsis. Then research agencies and their submission requirements and follow them; no wavering or you will be rejected. Once you create your wish list, call them and discuss the submission process. The navigation process to obtaining a literary is listed as follows.

1. Finish the manuscript.

2. Research representation in your genre.

3. Write the synopsis (usually the back blurb or Amazon description).

4. Craft the query letter that follows the standard format, opening paragraph introducing you and your book, second paragraph about the book, and closing statement with your contact information.

5. Send query letters.

6. Keep and maintain a spreadsheet that includes the agency, agent, the date you sent it, and their response.

Rejected?

A publishing company or literary agent often rejects your book, and they don't have to give you a reason. Ouch! If you are an author, chances are, somewhere along the line, you have received a rejection letter from a publisher or a literary agent. Don't take it as a sign of rejection, instead nod your head and keep it high as you just joined some of the best authors in the world who received rejection letters. Now, doesn't that make you feel better? Just think about the company you are now in. Look at the following authors whose manuscripts were rejected but authored extraordinary literature.

Louisa May Alcott – ***Little Women*** is a classic, but if Alcott had listened to her rejection, *"Stick to Teaching,"* we wouldn't have heard of this book that has shaped literature.

F. Scott Fitzgerald – I remember in high school when our English teacher told my class we would have to read ***The Great Gatsby***. I had never heard of it. Then one night at my grandmother's house, I was reading the book. She got so excited because it was one of her favorites. She went to her room and retrieved an autographed copy of it. Just think, the first publisher didn't like the book and suggested that Fitzgerald remove Gatsby as a character. The rest is history.

George Orwell – Have you ever heard of the novel ***Animal Farm?*** Who hasn't, right? However, if George Orwell had given up on his dream after receiving a rejection letter from the publishing company Faber & Faber, the history of this book would have been very different. Four publishing companies rejected this book because they didn't want to participate in the political satire business.

H. G. Wells – One of my favorite books of all time is the ***War of the Worlds***. It is also one of my favorite movies. When the first editor got a hold of this book, he hailed it as "An endless nightmare." I think the verdict would be, "Oh, don't read that horrid book." Horrid? I think not. His alien invasion book is still among the favorites for science fiction lovers.

Herman Melville – Have you ever heard of the book ***Moby Dick***? Talk about a whale of a story that almost didn't get published. Many publishers rejected this classic book. They didn't want to publish a book about a whale. One such company was Peter J. Bentley of Bentley & Son Publishing House that didn't want to publish a book about a whale but suggested, "First, we must ask, does it have to be a whale? We recommend an antagonist with a more popular visage among the younger readers. For instance, could not the Captain be struggling with depravity toward young, perhaps voluptuous, maidens?"

Melville didn't give up, and *Moby Dick* was published less than a month after it was rejected. So, the moral of this story is don't give up and keep writing.

I am the publisher who has sent my fair share of rejection letters to hungry aspiring authors. It wasn't easy knowing that they had put their heart and soul into writing their manuscript, but I had good reasons. Let me expand by addressing the top ten reasons for rejecting a manuscript for publication.

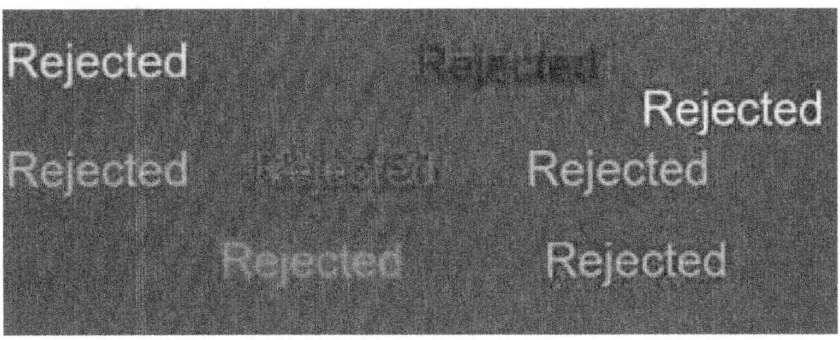

1. **The manuscript was full of grammatical, typographical errors, or otherwise junked.** You know you have a poorly written manuscript when you can't get past the opening sentence in the first chapter. Surprisingly enough, it

happens more often than I care to remember. I'll give you the perfect example.

> "The sun peeked as Thomas stood on the water's edge. His eyes flushed with tears as they fell to the ground."

What is wrong with that opener? Reread it to absorb the details. By the way, this is a real example. Do you see any grammatical errors? What about any typos? What about excess words? What about misused words? Bingo!

I honestly couldn't get over the third word, "Peeked." Misused words happen far more often than not. "Peeked" is the word to use if someone peeks inside a box, a room, or a refrigerator. Peak is used when something has made it to the top, as the sun peaked. Have I piqued your interest? It is important to locate these types of words that are often misused.

Now onto my next problem with the opener. Frankly, the author could have left it with "His eyes flushed." That's it. We know that when eyes flush, it's with tears. Next, we already know that tears travel downward; so, why the unnecessary words? Again, that's when editing comes in. It would have been far better for the author to have written something else about our character to draw us in. Here's the example.

> "The sun peaked as Thomas stood on the water's edge. His eyes flushed as his throat tightened. ***I can't believe she drowned; I miss her***.

2. **The author rambled on and on about unimportant things that didn't direct the plot or the character forward**. I

realize that as novelists, we must describe places, things, events, and characteristics of our characters. However, we don't have to go overboard and use two pages to describe a character's apartment or office or anything else. If you do, it gets wordy and has nothing to do with the story, and readers lose interest quickly. Don't bog your readers so much detail they can't enjoy the story. The essential things to include are sights, sounds, smells, something out-of-place or out of the norm, and possibly how something feels to the touch. That's far more attractive to readers.

3. **There was nothing new or attractive inside your novel.** It's essential to face the facts. There is a great deal of competition in all genres. If your novel comes across as I've read this before, then it's going to be rejected. Find new twists and turns and give your readers something they have never read.

4. **Your genre wasn't what that publisher specializes in.** For instance, I often receive self-help books. However, no matter how good one was written, the company I worked for only published non-fiction in all genres. Therefore, always do your research and submit to publishers specializing in your genre to avoid rejection.

5. **The author lived in their fantasy world.** Believe it or not, there is so much competition in the book market today that a publisher may not want to take a chance on you if you have no presence on social media. Trust me; once they get your book, they do a Google search on you. If they find you are active, that's a plus, unless you come across on the crazy side and bring that baggage with you. Watch what you post as we don care about your reputation. Do you constantly appear with a glass of wine in your hand with glazed-over eyes and slobbering drunk? No publisher wants to deal with a crazy drunk. Do you write racist comments are always demeaning others? Again, no

publisher wants to deal with that either. I'm just saying, this part of your career is in your hands. Remember, as an author, you are forming a brand, which is you.

6. **Oversold themselves, basically lying in their query letter**. It's one thing to toot your own horn, but to say you will be the best-selling author because your mother says so or because you write just like James Patterson or Anne Rice isn't doing yourself any favors. Also, don't claim you're an expert on something unless you are, then be able to back it up. If you have won a contest, make sure you did, don't put one down to pad the query letter. We look at those things as well.
7. **Once rejected, consider yourself rejected only by that publisher and not the world.** I say this because I have received countless letters asking me to take a second look. They beg, plead, or embarrass themselves with an unbecoming choice of words, including profanity. Seriously, move on. When I received those letters, not only did I throw them away, but I also had a file of DO NOT CONSIDER ANYTHING FROM THIS AUTHOR. Publishers are busy people and must be respected. What this also did was turn me off from accepting any revisions. Had the author written me a nice thank you note for my feedback and said I am taking courses, honing my skills, hiring a developmental editor, etc., they would have had my attention, and I would have likely read the revision.
8. **The author couldn't answer basic questions during a phone call such as who is your target audience, where do you see this book going, have you considered how you'll market the book?** If you aren't well-spoken on the phone, what makes me, as a publisher, think you are going to handle television or radio interviews?

9. **The book wasn't formatted correctly.** Bad and intolerable formatting is one of the greatest sins of a novelist. Need I say more?
10. **The pacing of the book was scattered.** It's hard to follow a book where you're jumping around within a scene. Make sure every scene you write has a beginning, middle, and end, including conflict. Don't bore your reader.

CHAPTER TWENTY-ONE

Marketing

Once their book is completed, one of the most challenging things for an author is to market it. We were born to be writers, not marketers. However, writers must become marketers if they stand a chance to compete with the millions of other books published. As an author, would you sit down to write your novel without the appropriate tools? I think not. Then why market your book without them? You shouldn't, as your marketing strategy will not be effective.

As an author who published traditionally and self-published, my goal has always been to sell my books and receive a high ranking on Amazon. I finally did it when I published my new novel, *Never Stop Running*. My goal was to have a street team to help me promote my book, get pre-sale orders, and maintain complete control of my book. The early buzz that my street team created worked as on the first day of publication, *Never Stop Running,* received the rank of #1 New Release on Amazon. Oh, happy day! Trust me when I say I was surprised because I did not have one review. So, what happened, and how did I do it?

What happened is easy; my pre-sales sent me to the top. I spent months marketing the book and making contacts. I took my time to make sure the book was professionally edited and had a striking cover. After this happened, several new authors reached out to me and asked how I accomplished this ranking. Here is my simplistic marketing strategy.

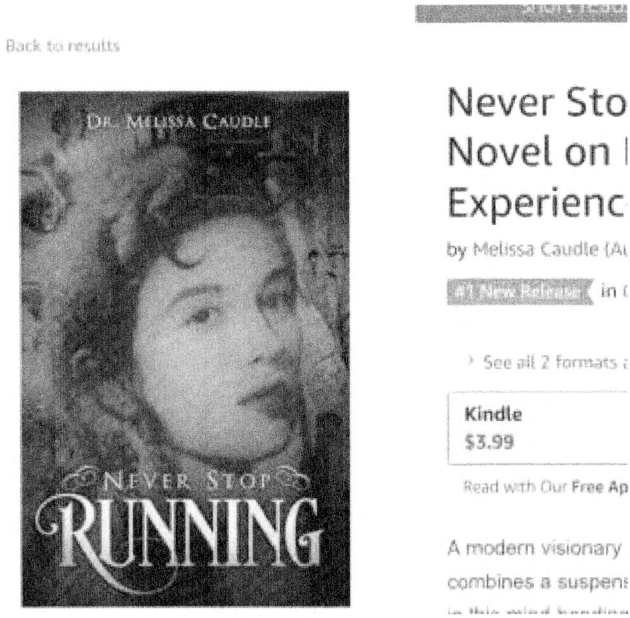

Author Website

I have been writing and publishing for almost two decades; so, I have developed a following. One of the first things I did as an author was to create an author website. Even if yours is only one page, develop it. Feel free to visit mine at www.drmelcaudle.com/.

What my website did for me was to give me a place to put every book, screenplay, and artwork in one place, whereby I merged my followers. I'm not only a novelist, but I also have 'How to' books for screenwriters and adult coloring books I illustrated. This crossover played a role, and my fans see me as a real person. Therefore, I strongly recommend developing an author's website before publishing your first book. Then, as you publish more, your website can grow.

There are certain must-haves for your author's website. These include:

- Your Bio – write it in the third person and highlight your accomplishments.
- A professional photograph.
- A link to subscribe or to follow you.
- A page for your book.
- A page for your press releases.
- A Media Kit page for journalists and bloggers to download information on you and your book. This kit should include what I call a one-pager or sell sheet, information about your book, your contact information, and where the book can be purchased.

Landing Page

Every book you publish needs its own landing page. If you go to my website, you will see the landing pages for *Never Stop Running*, *The Keystroke Killer*, and A.D.A.M. I will create a landing page for Secret Romances: A Forbidden Thirst for Love when it is time. My other books for screenwriters, actors, and colorists are on one page on my website, as they are a specific genre and niche. Below is my landing page on my website.

Blog

You are a writer, so write; easier said than done. I have been writing my blog for years, developing a following. I have millions in readership, so I make sure I consistently blog. I'll admit there were a couple of years when I was ill and didn't blog, but the blog itself remained. Then, I could pick up where I left off.

Suppose you don't have a blog, guest blog on someone else's. I frequently guest blog on others to cross-promote. I believe in supporting other authors. If you review my blog, you'll notice that I promote other authors' books. Why? Because of what I call cross-linking. I promote a book by another author in my blog or on my sidebar. Then, when fans search for their name or book, my blog comes up with my books. So, don't be afraid to promote other authors' books.

Goodreads and Bookbub

Start your author pages on these sites as soon as possible and keep your information accurate. I especially love the feature on Goodreads that allows readers to ask me questions. I have garnished reviews and generated sales that way because they saw me as a real person. Also, be sure to claim your author page.

Social Media

Don't be afraid to post the stages of your writing on your social media sites. When I wrote *The Keystroke Killer: Transcendence,* I informed my friends and followers what was going on every step of the way. I did the same thing with *Never Stop Running.* I released the covers of my books, and I told them what progress I made during the Beta Read stages.

I reached out and shared my milestones across many social media platforms, including Facebook, Twitter, and Instagram.

Book Launch or Street Team

One thing I learned; you can't promote a book by yourself. You need a dedicated team to help you spread the word. My team formed naturally. At first, my team included my family, friends, publisher, editors, and beta readers. These people are essential to help you launch your book or generate pre-sales. Eventually, I fostered several fans who loved my books and wanted to help through my blog. To make sure your street team works for you, do not take them for granted. Thank them constantly and give them free copies of your book. I also include in my acknowledgment section, my beta readers, and editors. They work hard for us and need to be thanked. The more members on your team, the more promotion your book gets. Team members push my notifications on Facebook and share my posts.

Book Reviews

Honest book reviews are important, but they are tough to get. However, I have found a clever site that will aid you in getting book reviews. Arc Bookends will help you by sending your book to reviewers for free. In exchange, they agree to review your book. Visit them at: https://arc.booksends.com/. Also, find other authors on your social media sites and agree to review their book, honestly, in exchange for them to review yours. Ask your launch team and beta readers to leave a review for you too.

Note: My novel *Never Step Running* opened *as* the #1 New Release on Amazon with no reviews. It is important to know that your ranking isn't based on reviews but on the number of books you sell.

Provide Excerpts of Next Book in Published Book

There is nothing like giving your fans a tease about what is coming up next. When I published *The Keystroke Killer: Transcendence*, on October 31, 2018, at the end of the book (in publishing terms, it is called back matter); I provided excerpts for my subsequent two novels, *Never Stop Running,* released January 19, 2019, and

A.D.A.M. released in June 2019. I also include ads for my other books in the back matter. What if you already published a book, and you didn't include an excerpt in it for your next one? Add it immediately.

Know Your Niche Audience

I'm not speaking about knowing only one of your niche audiences because every one of my books has its own. At least I know that; so, I market to that audience when I market a book. That is the key to the success of a book in terms of pre-sales.

Reach Out to Social Influencers

You can quickly go broke advertising and marketing your book as an author. If you don't have a large following, see if someone who does will help you out. I'll be honest with you; I have a considerable following, and other authors have benefited from it. One of the best examples is the first-time authors who hire me to edit their books. When they add my name to the credits as an editor, and someone researches my name on Amazon, their books come up too. If you don't believe me, go to Amazon and search "Dr. Melissa Caudle." Look at how many other books come up, like *One Step at a Time* by Liz Havrilla and Dr. L.A. Davis' book, *So You Want to be a Doctoral Learner! Are You Nuts?* or *Where the Mind Wanders* by Jamie Alyson or *The Mysteries of Woodland Academy* by Kirhonda Williams. I am their editor, and they benefit from my following. So, a small plug, I also edit; and I am one of the senior editors with Absolute Author Publishing House. If you need an editor, email me at drmelcaudle@gmail.com.

Author Interviews

I cannot stress enough how essential author interviews are. When you are interviewed, you immediately get a backlink to add to your author's website. This helps in the rankings. In addition, there are various author interviews, e.g., written for blogs, radio, podcasts, television, and YouTube. Do them and do as many as you can.

Email Marketing

One of the best email marketing tools is to email your subscribers. I use MailChimp and my marketing tool on GoDaddy to send out marketing blasts to my subscribers and followers on my blog and my website. If you haven't started a subscription list, do it immediately. It took me at least five years to gather these subscribers. I authored two books to help you with marketing.

1. *How to Launch and Market a Book: The Six Month Countdown* available on Amazon in eBook, paperback, and audio.

2. *How to Write a Logline to Increase Sales: Everything an Author Should Know but Wasn't Told about Loglines for Nonfiction and Fiction Books* available on Amazon in eBook, paperback, and audio.

Marketing Tools

I can't say enough about marketing tools for an author, which include the one-pager, press releases, ads, and book trailers. I get tons of emails and messages from people who view my book trailers. Also, I have effectively used *The Keystroke Killer.* I had ten different trailers and at least five for Never Stop Running. People like videos. The key here is I provided a variety of book trailers.

Here is what you need to market your book effectively.

One Sheet

An one sheet is a single document that highlights your book that you should have available to give to book reviewers, newspapers, magazines, bookstore managers, etc. Your business card isn't effective as it lacks the information needed. The most important items to include in your one sheet are:

- Your Name,
- The Book's Name and the Book's Cover,
- The Book's Genre,
- Catchy Headline,
- Three paragraphs – 1. Introduce yourself 2. Introduce Book 3. Call to Action – Where to purchase the book,
- Contact Information, and
- Email address, phone number, and author website.

A Flipbook Trailer

A flipbook trailer is a twenty to thirty-second video that highlights the elements of your book. They are vital as they give readers a chance to look inside your book for the format and style, and it is the perfect opportunity to showcase what other readers think about your book. Here are several examples of flipbook trailers from different genres of books I authored.

How to Launch and Market a Book - https://youtu.be/un3T28RK6zo

Never Stop Running - https://youtu.be/hksXq0PRJag

How to Write a Logline to Increase Sales - https://youtu.be/xbDPSYkt8f4

A Book Trailer

Long are the days when someone will pick up your book because of the front cover. Yes, that is important. However, readers want to be drawn into your book visually, and a book trailer is the perfect means to accomplish this. Think of your book trailer as if it were a film. When creating a book trailer, make sure it is catchy and meets the tone and genre of your book. As crazy as this may sound, do a viral video ad for your book, and post it to your Facebook site and YouTube. Get creative and use your imagination. If you don't have the capability of creating your own, we have a team of film producers and graphic artists who can help you with a concept. Look at a couple of video ads below I created for my book *The Keystroke Killer: Transcendence*. Notice how different they are as they are designed for different reasons. What I accomplished here is targeting my audience in fun and creative ways. These ads caught my readers' attention before they knew they were about a novel, and I capitalized on dog owners, cat owners, and happy dancers.

Cinematic Trailer: https://youtu.be/v_Lr7DDtOwA

Audience Niche Trailer: https://youtu.be/u7i11DMDZPs

Audience Niche Trailer/Dog Lovers - https://youtu.be/jjCt-Fnl1sI

Branding Trailer: https://youtu.be/LxB0Y6Y5V7M

Notice that each trailer focuses on something different and targets a different audience. That is the goal of effective trailers.

TIP 15: To view hundreds of book trailers from cover reveals to flipbooks to cinematic, visit my YouTube site playlist below.

https://www.youtube.com/playlist?list=PL0wanuK3PsWCSGbaLTuforvW14kkXxjf4

Author Website

An author's website is a must. With that said, if you have a website, be sure to backlink any press releases, trailers, and author interviews. It will increase views as well as increase your SEO ranking. I use GoDaddy to host my websites and use their templates to create them. The template I use is called Mint. Also, plenty of Fiverr freelancers can design websites at reasonable prices. Check them out.

Book Reviews

Book reviews are a must, and I don't mean the ones your friends and family write for you on Amazon. Although they are essential, having a professional reviewer is key. Why? When you have a professional reviewer read and review your book, it carries weight with your readers.

Press Release

Don't underestimate the power of a press release. Not only will a press release give your book coverage, but it will also get your name and your book into listings for web searches. The more press, the better your book sells.

Book Tour

Authors must meet the readers who purchase their books. Sometimes the cost of travel is a forbidden factor. However, consider hosting an online book tour and publicizing it on Facebook. This is where all the other marketing materials are needed to advertise and promote your tour.

Author Blogging

Yes, blogging is important. Unfortunately, many authors don't use this resource to promote their writing because they don't have the time to maintain a blog. This is a perfect answer to your blogging problem. You can be a guest blogger as much or as little as you want. This is a wonderful way to share with your readers, and it gives you backlinks. So, what are you waiting for? Become a guest blogger and social media influencer today.

Tweet About Your Book

You can reach hundreds of potential readers by tweeting your book's information. So, don't miss this opportunity. The key to tweeting is to do it often, if not daily, and be sure to use your hashtags. Hashtags are important as they help to draw potential readers to your subject.

Use Social Media to Promote Your Book

Get on as many social media sites as you can. Readers love the personal human factor. So, allow them to get to know you as a person and not just as an author. Use Facebook, Goodreads, Twitter, and Pinterest, effectively and often. Don't just advertise your book; let them get to know you.

Create an Email Signature

A simple and free method to advertise your book is to create a specialized email signature that includes your author's website, a small ad about your book, and a link to purchase your book.

Take Your Book to Your Readers

This is where a large purse or backpack comes in handy. You can't sell your books when you're out and about if you don't have one with you. Of course, you can always guide your readers to the Amazon page and have them purchase the book immediately, but there is nothing better than having your book on hand and offering to autograph it for them. Again, this brings out the human factor, and readers love an autographed copy.

Set Up at Craft Fairs, Book Fairs, and Other Types of Shows

Again, it is important that you, as an author, are seen and interact with the public. Craft fairs are perfect for this. A more expensive approach, and only if it fits your genre, get a small booth at Comicon. You meet thousands of people who want to meet you.

Start an Email List

Stay connected with your readers and start an email list. Then, as you write and publish more books, you will have an automatic list to promote them. The easiest way I have found is to use Mailchimp. It is free for the first 2,000 subscribers. Then, once a week, send an email. Don't push your book; let it sell itself. But share other things like book reviews, your book tour, or write a short story and include it in it.

CHAPTER TWENTY-TWO

Reviews

Whether you check your books' online reviews daily or haven't even bothered to claim your author websites on Author Central, Goodreads, and Bookbub, readers are reviewing your book. In addition, potential readers and fans are reading what others are saying about you online. In a survey by YouGov.com, they reported that 79% of U.S. adult Internet users check online reviews before they purchase a book.

The second thing they do is read the book's blurb or synopsis. That is how essential reviews, and your synopsis, are to your book's sales. As authors, we all dream of having nothing but five star-reviews because they are a powerful way to drive readers to purchase your book. So we go out of the way to encourage our friends, family, and colleagues to leave a review, and then someone we don't know leaves a terrible review crushing your inner author soul.

A fellow author I follow recently asked me what he should do because he received a negative review? Do you ignore it? Do you address it?

You will have to do something because one in thirty-three authors report that the sales of their book dropped after a negative review. Ouch! All your hard work went down the drain. Your chances are low that you will receive a bad review. However, many authors ignore online review sites because they're terrified of getting a bad review. If this is you, take comfort because another recent survey reports that just one in twenty-five entrepreneurs say a negative online review has impacted them. Chances are low, but bad reviews happen. If someone negatively reviews your book online, how should you respond?

Here are the dos and don'ts of dealing with negative online reviews.

Negative Online Reviews – The "Don'ts"

Here are the "Don'ts" of dealing with a negative review of your book.

1. **Don't take it personally.** I know it is hard not to take any negative review or comment personally, but you can't. Remember, they are not reviewing you but are reviewing the words you wrote. When you receive a book review, it is a subjective review, not about you as a person but about the book's contents.
2. **Don't get defensive.** The first time they receive a negative review, many authors feel defeated, and then they get angry and defensive. Wait! That might be the natural thing to do, but it isn't the best thing to do. One negative

comment by you and your entire authoring career can be over in an instant. I am a firm believer that authors don't get in trouble for what they haven't said or written; they get in trouble when they respond angrily, which sets up a viral infestation of your good book. Respond positively and not defensively. You might offer a clarification. However, never belittle the reviewer, shame them, or rub them the wrong way, because it will only worsen the situation. Remember, you are the professional author and that you are a business.

3. **Don't ignore it.** It is almost as bad as posting a defensive statement when you ignore a negative online review. First, an ignored negative review validates the reviewer because you failed to address the issue. Second, potential readers question whether you even care. If you don't care, why should they? Third, being unresponsive also demonstrates that you might not be an authentic author. Finally, people love to interact with authors and get to know them through blogs and social media posts.

4. **Don't participate in an online battle**. Trolls! Trolls! Trolls! Sometimes, you can do nothing about a troll who loves to be involved in negative confrontations. Don't engage with Trolls. Your readers are smart enough to know the difference between a Troll and an honest negative review. Your goal in dealing with a Troll is to restate the facts and then calmly move on to another topic. Your readers will identify that you are responding as a professional.

5. **Don't go on a campaign to beg for positive reviews.** There is something not right for an author who begs for positive reviews or purchases them from various freelance sites. These reviews stick out like a sore thumb and will backfire on an author. Don't fall victim to this unprofessional way of dealing with a bad negative review. Often, future readers are turned off immediately to your book because of what they deem as unethical behavior of an author. The best

review for your book is an unsolicited, honest review. Those stand out to future readers more than the negative review.

6. **Forget about the review.** Make yourself a promise that after you examine the review and retrieve any reliable information to help you become a better writer, you'll forget the review. That's right, never reread it. Don't go there. It is in the past, and that is where it should remain.

Negative Online Reviews – The "Dos"

Responding unprofessionally or unethically to a negative book review could cause significant damage to your career. Listed below are my suggestions for responding to a negative review online.

1. **Honesty is the best policy.** It is the best policy to always be honest in all dealings in life. Your word becomes a bond that your readers can trust. Most reviewers who leave a negative review are leaving their honest opinion. They may not have liked your character, the plot, or how you wrote. It is their opinion; honor that. Everyone is entitled to their opinion. When you receive a negative review, respond by thanking that reviewer for their opinion and that you will reflect on their feedback. Then thank them for purchasing your book and for supporting authors, and you genuinely regret that your book did not meet their entertainment style. In this manner, you are not blaming them, bashing them, or criticizing them. When your readers read your response, they recognize you are a fair and unbiased person who conducts themselves without reproach. Also, any message should be authentic.
2. **Promote a positive image of your book.** In a separate post without mentioning the negative review or reviewer, promote your book with an ad that includes reviews and quotes from positive reviewers. I would even issue a press

release about how well the book is selling and announce any future books you plan on writing. Put out at least ten to one positive press and posts to a negative one. Many blogs review books or interview authors, such as Absolute Author Publishing House and my blog. Take advantage of these. Also, flood your social media sites with a new book trailer and hold the world premiere on Facebook to generate interest and create your own YouTube videos or podcasts describing your book, your writing process, and a variety of interviews. I would also conduct a book Giveaway immediately on a social media influencer's blog.

3. **Grow and Learn from a Negative Review.** A negative review can be something positive if you allow it to happen. How? You must grow and become a better author honing your craft. If you have only received one negative review, you might not need to do much growing. Also, research who the review is from. Do they constantly post negative reviews, or are their reviews a mixture of positive and negative? A mixture indicates that they are giving their unbiased opinion. However, if you continually receive negative reviews, learn to isolate what the reviewers tell you about your writing. Determine if there are any patterns and address them in your writing style. Also, this is the time to review your manuscript. Did you have it professionally edited and formatted? Is it written in a difficult language? Are there plot holes? Again, honesty is the best policy, and you have to be honest with yourself. I have published dozens of nonfiction and fiction books, and I learn something new with each one. I stay on top of the latest publishing trends; I read other authors' novels; I edit other authors' novels professionally. All of this makes me a better writer, and the more efficient you become, you will write better books, which lowers your risk for any negative review.

I hope you find solace that a negative review isn't the ending for your book. It means that your book is getting read and by people who care enough to leave a comment just as much as you cared enough to write it. A bad review is not doom and gloom but the time for an author to take the higher road. When you do, you'll be stronger for it, and others will recognize it.

CHAPTER TWENTY-THREE

Hot off the Press

After you publish your book, your work has just begun; consider yourself a PR specialist. I hate to be the bearer of bad news, but you must market your book. I have over eighteen years of experience in writing and publishing press releases. I have found that authors have difficulty constructing two things -- their synopsis for their book and their press release.

To be clear, you must understand the purpose of a press release. Although I include it as a marketing tool, it serves other purposes.

1. To get the attention of journalists for additional interviews.

2. To get your name and book in the news.

3. Generate publicity.

4. Increases an author's branding awareness.

5. To announce the publication of your book.

6. Builds search engine traffic.

So, what is the key to writing a powerful press release? Include all parts of a press release which include:

- The Heading & The Subtitle
- Introductory Paragraph
- The Main Body – the who, what, when, where, why, etc.
- About the Author or About Us if you co-authored a book
- Contact information

The Heading

Your heading is your title.

The key to writing a powerful press release is to target your readers with a specific headline for your book. It must grab the attention of your reader or a journalist because that is the first thing they see. Therefore, your heading must be straight to the point and short. This is not the time to get wordy. Also, consider using a headline that is catchy to grab the reader's attention. After that, you need a subtitle, maybe a complete sentence that summarizes your press release.

The Introductory Paragraph

Bloggers, media influencers, and journalists are busy and don't have time to read a massive amount of information. In a powerful press release, less is better. Get to the point right away and provide something interesting to keep them reading. Omit rift-raft and long details in your opening paragraph.

The Main Body

Now it is time to tell them about your novel. Your synopsis is excellent because it explains what your book is about. Remember to use the old-fashioned writing technique and include the who, what, where, when, and why? You could also begin or end your main body with your logline. Last, include the reviewer's comments and quotes.

About the Author

When you write this section, it should be boilerplate. One mainstay for an author is to have a powerful biography. Use it here and save yourself valuable time.

Contact Information

When you use a press release service, you must include your contact information by law. This gets a little scary for some authors because they have to provide their home address and phone number. Don't let that scare you, as Absolute Author has a press release service that is reasonable and cost-effective. They can issue your press release under their name.

A Little Extra Oomph

Many press release sites don't allow the use of images; however, when you send it to journalists and bloggers, be sure to include them. In addition, I suggest you include the cover of your book and your sell sheet. I'm including a press release I developed so you can identify the parts I wrote about in this blog. Immediately following, I have included a template for your use. Use these as a guideline when you write your press release. Then, if all fails, contact me for a small service. Then I can write and distribute your press release.

PRESS RELEASE

January 24, 2019

NEVER STOP RUNNING DEBUTS AS #1 NEW RELEASE

Never Stop Running the novel by Dr. Melissa Caudle is her second novel and launched as the #1 New Release on Amazon.

New Orleans, LA – Absolute Author Publishing House is proud to debut a new novel, "Never Stop Running," from Dr. Melissa Caudle which launched as the #1 New Release on Amazon.

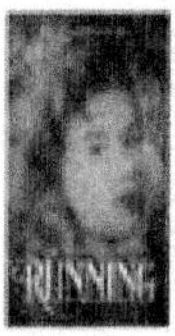

A modern visionary and one of the newest authors to come from America, Dr. Melissa Caudle combines a suspenseful thriller and the search for truth in regard to past lives and reincarnation in this mind-bending novel in the tradition of "*This Body: A Novel of Reincarnation*" by Laurel Doud, "*Journey of Souls*," by Michael Newton, and Past Lives, "*Many Masters*" by Brian L. Weiss. The result is a masterful original fiction novel as profound as it is awe inspiring. "*Never Stop Running*" is a page-turning thriller that begs to be read in a single sitting as this mental time travel spanning centuries and numerous past lives through regression hypnotherapy unfolds. Based on a true story of one woman's struggle to recover her memories after a devastating accident left her with retrograde amnesia. This is an astonishing novel from an unforgettable author and is a must read.

What Others Are Saying

"Based on real events of regression hypnotic sessions of one brave woman, this is a tale of destiny and soul mates not to be missed. The most intriguing book you'll read all year." Dr. Carol Michaels

"You don't have to believe in reincarnation to enjoy this tale, but it will get you to thinking about the possibility." Erin Wright

"A masterful novel that keeps you engaged. A must read." Tina Rahin

ABOUT THE AUTHOR

Dr. Melissa Caudle debuted her novel Never Stop Running: A Novel on Reincarnation as the #1 New Release on Amazon. She is best known for her book The Keystroke Killer Transcendence, a psychological thriller which took her to death row to interview serial killers. Her books have received starred reviews in Publishers Weekly, BookBub, Goodreads and on Amazon. She also writes non-fiction for screenwriters, novelists or film producers and has a series of adult coloring books called Abstract Faces. She enjoys the city life of New Orleans along with her husband Mike and their two sidekicks, a Tuxedo cat named Meow Mix and an American Gray Shorthair named Simone. When she is not writing, she composes music, draws, paints, reads or edits other author's books. Her goal is to continue to live a full and rich life and write every day.

If you want to know when her next book will come out, please visit her website at http://www.drmelcaudle.com or https://www.drmelcaudle.blogspot.com where you can sign up to receive an email when she has her next release.

PRESS RELEASE TEMPLATE

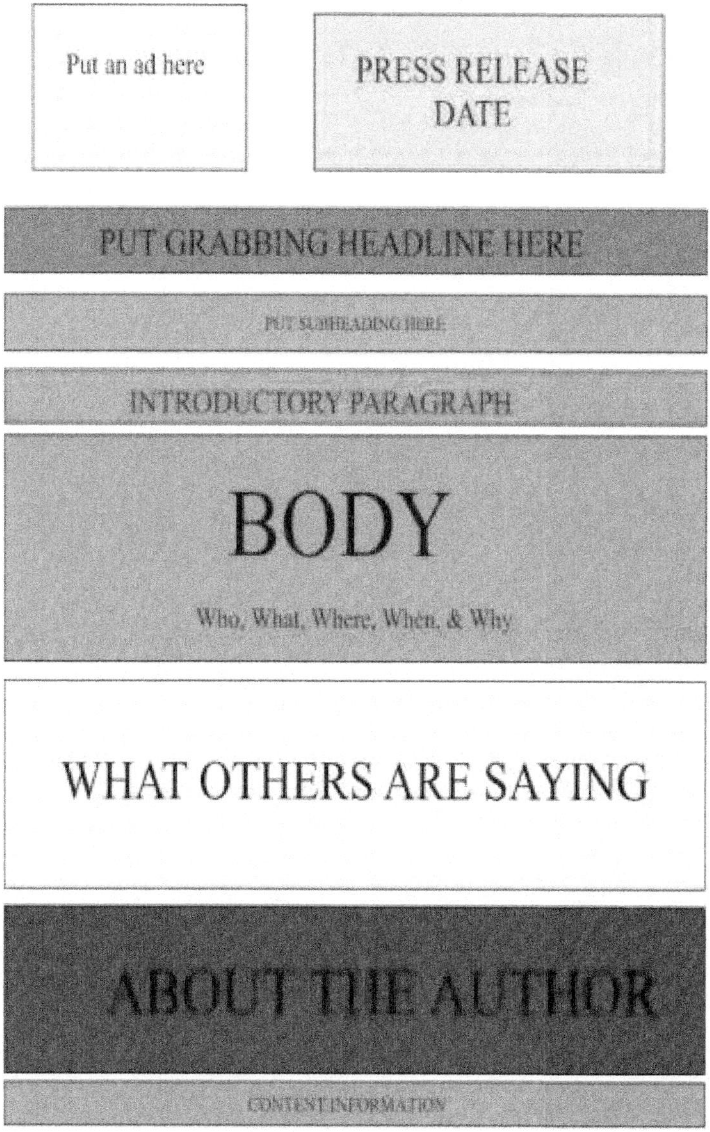

I hope you found the information in this book beneficial. Check out my other writing books on Amazon that can help you become a successful author.

Happy writing!

ABOUT THE AUTHOR

Dr. Melissa Caudle earned a Ph.D. in statistical research and administration from the University of New Orleans, Master's of Education and Administration from Stephen F. Austin State University, and a Bachelor's degree in Special Education from the University of Texas. She is a retired award-winning high school principal, central office administrator, and has taught at Loyola University in New Orleans, LA. She came into the television and film production arena in 1986 when she was on the morning news with a live episode talk-format segment dealing with educational issues for children. Capitalizing on her educational training and background, she uses her experience and training to give her readers easy-to-understand yet comprehensive information. Her books for screenwriters, producers, reality show creators, and novelists are fast becoming the number of resources around the globe.

Dr. Mel is also a feature and documentary filmmaker, including *Mexico Missions*, *The Dolphins in Terry Cove*, *The Alabama Gulf Coast Zoo*, *Sean Kelly's Irish Pub*, *Beauvoir,* and *Voices of the*

Innocent. Her film credits include producer on the independent film *Dark Blue, The Creek Dweller in the Bayou, Ombre Ma Fi,* and associate producer on *Varla Jean and the Mushroomheads* and *Girls Gone Gangsta*. In addition, Dr. Mel has worked on films such *STRAW DOGS* starring Kate Bosworth, James Marsden, James Woods, and Alexander Skarsgard; *MARDI GRAS* starring Carmen Electra and Josh Gad; *On the Seventh Day* with Blair Underwood, Pam Grier, and Jamie Alyson; and *Dirty Politics* starring Melissa Peterman, Beau Bridges, and Judd Nelson. She also has been a program director for a television station in Alabama. Her company, On the Lot Productions, LLC, is currently in pre-production on several feature films. In addition, she has won over thirty-five screenwriting contests. Dr. Mel currently lives in New Orleans, LA, and is married to Mike Caudle. She has three daughters, three sons-in-law, and is the proud grandmother of six grandsons and one granddaughter. When she is not writing, she composes music, draws, and goes on cruises.

Publishing Services Offered by Dr. Mel

Professional Editing
Formatting
Marketing
Author Interviews (written and on Zoom)
Coaching on Writing
Coaching on Distribution

To book Dr. Mel for your publishing and marketing needs, visit her Fiverr Dashboard at:

https://www.fiverr.com/melissacaudle?up_rollout=true

Tell her you purchased this book, and she'll give you a discount.

How to Launch and Market a Book: The Six-Month Countdown

by Melissa Caudle (Author)

From the #1 New Release Author, Dr. Melissa Caudle, comes the secrets of launching and publishing a book as an independent author. Why waste hundreds of hours trying to find this information or spend hundreds of dollars on webinars? Have you been there and done that? This book is an essential resource for authors who desire to have their book reach the #1 New Release as it provides specific steps during the pre-launch of a book six months out to marketing it once it is released. The advice and steps supplied throughout the book are golden. If you are an author, you need this book. Order your copy today.

How to Write a Logline to Increase Sales: Everything an Author Should Know but Wasn't Told about Loglines for Nonfiction and Fiction Books

by Dr. Melissa Caudle (Author)

"How to Write a Logline for Your Book to Increase Sales" is considered a must-have for authors in the publishing industry. The reason -- to grab the attention of potential readers, you must present your novel or book in a complete marketing package that includes the logline. A powerful, attention-grabbing logline aids in increasing the sale potential of your book, which means more royalties. Dr. Carol Michaels, CEO of Absolute Author Publishing House, said, "When authors can't narrow what their book is about in one sentence, it makes me question the rest of their manuscript. I always ask authors to submit a minimum of five different loglines because it tells me a lot about their writing style, and I learn about the book. Readers are no different. That's how important a powerful logline is." Too often, authors can't move from their concept that takes up hundreds of pages in their manuscript to a single sentence. When asked, "What is your book about?" authors often stammer and begin the answer by describing either the character or the plot. That's not ideal, as the message you're trying to deliver becomes a jumbled mess. Without an attention-getting logline, your book will swim with sharks in the middle of the ocean without a chance to grab the reader's attention. When this happens, your sales plummet. Do you want to increase the sales of your book? Of course, you do. Do you have trouble writing an attention-grabbing logline? If you said, "Yes," this book is for you. Written by a #1 New Release Amazon author, the information in this book guides an author in writing a compelling logline.

If you found this book helpful, I would appreciate leaving me an honest review on Amazon and my Goodreads page. Authors always appreciate the feedback.

INDEX

Printed in Great Britain
by Amazon

78651026R00149